First published in Great Britain in 1992 by
POETRY NOW
4 Hythegate, Werrington,
Peterborough, PE4 7ZP

Foreword

Poppy Fields

This century has been one of the most turbulent in history, having witnessed two major world wars and numerous conflicts on smaller but no less significant scales.

Shifts in political fortunes and the ever changing balance of world power has forced nation after nation into confrontation. Unprecedented technological advances have also placed in the hands of antagonists the capability of invasion and mass destruction.

Of all the books of poetry dealing with war published over the years, this book is in a class of its own.

In July of this year, readers of the journal of The Royal British Legion were invited to submit work for possible inclusion in this anthology. Legion readers had been asked to contribute because many had first hand experience of war or friends and family at war.

Of the hundreds of poems received 176 were finally selected for publication in 'Poppy Fields', a fitting tribute to the sacrifices made by so many men and women during times of war.

The poems illustrate the horror of conflict both at home and on foreign soil and convey memories of heroism and hardship.

Above all, this book provides a valuable insight into what war means to us all.

Royalties from sales of Poppy Fields will be paid to the Royal British Legion.

Contents

B.E.F 1939 - 1940

We did not go for glory to the wars.
No conscious sense of duty did we bear,
No great thoughts moved us on our marching way,
No flame inflamed: no patriotic flare.

We knew our numbers, kept our rifles clean,
Despite encumbering gas masks, sang our songs,
Thinking but little what a war could mean
And ignorant about its rights and wrongs.

So mostly we did nothing more than wait
In readiness, and moved from there to here.
Sometimes our orders came by change, and late.
We dealt out death sometimes and lived in fear.

We came back not in triumph from the wars,
But thankfully, having had much to learn,
Remembering those, so young, who with us went,
But sadly, with us never did return.

Austin Shorney Gunner 53rd (City of London) H.A.A. Regt. R.A., T.A

Normandy

Come and stand in memory
of men who fought and died
they gave their lives in Normandy
Remember them with Pride

Soldiers, Airmen, Sailors
Airborne and Marines
who in Civvy life were Tailors
and men who worked Machines

British and Canadians
and men from USA
Forces from the Commonwealth
they all were there that day

To Juno, Sword and Utah
Beaches of Renown
also Gold and Omahah
that's where the ramps went down

The battle raged in Normandy
many lives were lost
the war must end in Victory
and this must be the cost

When my life is over
and I reach 'The Other Side'
I'll meet my friends from Normandy
and shake their hands with Pride

C Crain

Red Beret

Into an inferno those angels fell
The bridge at Arnhem was there objective,
Honest brave they para'd down
But the General's plans were defect.

Forward they pushed to foot of the bridge
Only to find they could go no further.
Now at the other side
Reinforced heavy armour

They waited in vain.
Fighting all the time.
For help that was promised.
But never came.

Pushed back fighting all the way
surrender, never entering there head,
for the beret's worn that day
were red.

H Pusey

Walking Wounded - 1943

We sat in dainty groups of three
Politely sipping tepid tea,
As aged parson's wife, our host
Poured out her chatter aimlessly
And offered cubes of ancient toast.

'The shortages in time of war
Affect us all, the rich and poor
And wives and mothers suffer too
(As Mister Churchill said today,)
To win the war and see it through'

'You should be thankful.' now she said
'To leave your hospital and bed
And, once your well and free from pain,
(You soldier-boys are fit and strong),
What joy at going back again.'

Gordon Charkin

Posthumous

Will you be born a restless one, I wonder,
Since she who carries you works at the wheel
Here where the hammers dominantly thunder
Rivet on rivet into the tensed steel?

Or will your spirit take from days hereafter -
Peace-days when apple-blossom's on the wing, -
Her quiet self, compact of peace and laughter,
Mould of contentment? We shall see, in Spring.

He who so passionately loves Spring's coming,
Who fathered you - the child he will not see -
He too was restless... to the end of roving,
Yet died content, that others might be free.

B O'Neil

ADC92

Ode to a Soldier

When the golden sun sinks in the West
And another day, draws to its close.
The stars come out to greet the night
And men should rest in sweet repose.

But do they get it? I'll say not,
A mans work is just begun.
To stand on guard, in bitter cold,
And wait for Gerry, with his gun,

Then when his two hours guard is Oe'r.
He goes to push his next relief.
Sighing loud, he gets down to it,
To get some sleep, is his belief.

If God consents he sleeps at last
Until the last relief, comes round.
And shouts 'Stand To' with all his might
A really truly awful sound.

Then standing there, stone cold once more.
He waits for the first pale light of dawn.
And says a prayer of thanks to God
That he's there to see another morn.

Written during the siege of Tobruk October 1941

W Slaney

The Battle of Britain

1940, and Britain stands alone
Breathless behind her moat she licks her wounds
Her allies scattered and her army smashed
Both friends and enemies now think she's doomed

The Nazi legions gather on the shores of France
As have others many time before
The supermen have Europe in their grasp
And wait a madman's word to give the final blow

Yet one more task remains ere this command be given
The Luftwaffe first must clear the sky
Before their tanks can roll 'round Piccadilly
Britain's thin blue line of airmen all must die

From Calais to Cherbourg the eagles gather
Here's chivalry perverted for a crooked cross
Theirs the way, the will, the means to conquer
Siegfried's sword unsheathed to give the Coup-de-Grace

So Goering's Ariel Armada tries it's hand
and Nazi wings blot out the summer sun
But Mitchell's dream, by Merlin powered, is ready
And for this foe, a deadlier Hurricane

Like that earlier Armada they are scattered
By the few who never paused to count the cost
But flew and fought as if the odds were mattered
To save an island that the whole world though was lost

James Sims

German Prisoners of War - Antwerp, 1944

In a courtyard of the shelled farm they stand,
The dusty mirrors of defeated eyes
Obscuring those proud days of fierce 'Sieg Heils!'
They droop, dispirited, parched of all hope,
Their faces black with battered Europe's dust,
Dark with prophecy of hearts' forebodings.
Against the crumbling walls their arms are stacked,
Neat mounds, packages of surrendered death.
Our guns, now mute, mime articulation,
Persuasive signposts to captivity.
'Où est le Bosche?' is chalked upon our truck,
Releasing Belgian shouts and plausive hands.
We sway our victor's way through the faint light:
They say we'll be in Antwerp for tonight.

W G Holloway

The Dislike of the Unlike

Will there ever on this earth be peace?
When will the dislike of the unlike cease?
When will men love, instead of hate?
Must we to strangers ever close the gate?

Can't we with other races strive to live;
Accept with grace, whatever they may give;
And if their customs very different be,
Perhaps of us, they think the same, may be?

Their way of worship is a different way;
For does it really matter how men pray?
The only difference is a way of life,
So must that difference bring eternal strife?

P May

The Heavens are Quiet Tonight ...

The heavens are quiet tonight
No pulsing beat of unleashed power
To break the silence, of a world
That lies in sleep ...
The stars are bright, where once
Hour by hour, a myriad twinkling lights
Foretold the passing of an aerial fleet
O'er a darkened world ...
The moons great golden orb sails on
No shadowy fleeting wing
Now mars her placid face
The whole night long ...
Yet, as I gaze thro' the still night
I seem to hear again, that sound
Of motors climbing, bearing high
The boys I knew ...
I lift my eyes, I search the skies
The stars are still as bright ...
We owe a debt, to those who gave ...
That the heavens are quiet ... *to night* ...

To my brother Fl/Sg I C Redfearn DFM
of 35 (Pathfinder) Sqdr.

J Redfearn

ARMISTICE
NOVEMBER · ELEVENTH
DAY · 1918

Remembrance Days

Remembrance day's they come and pass
Same old scene's same old cast
Pomp and pageantry all is there
Massed bands playing fill the air
For a moment time stands still
Bloodshed carnage men have had their fill
Then all is over we forget our pain
And for those who died did they die in vain

D Ryan

On Salisbury Plain

after another raid

This was the worst, when they had killed our women;
those gentle souls whose place was at the crib.
We laid them in a row quite neat and seemly,
striving to hold-back our sobs of woe.

Mid brown; like dolls; their shoes were neat
and pointed; right-angled rightly to the square.
Stilled, in a final mute attention, with all their
wealth of woman lying there.

Alive, we'd looked at them with longing;
touched them at the dances, held their hands.
Such sweet respite from trance of barracks marching;
a saneness from a peaceful land.

Now. shapely dull-dun ankles stilled and lifeless;
those lovely calves relaxed down in the dust;
her curves swelled-out 'gainst Army's buttoned pockets;
that polished brass an insult to their kind.

Oh, the evils that men never will unwind!

A Rowell

14

World War II

'Forth they went'
On to Battle they went
They hardly knew
How to hold a gun
But forth they went
With fear in their hearts
Dunkirk was fierce
And Bloody
Grenades flying
Around them
Every one trying to get
Into the boats to safety
But Bombs falling
Everywhere
Dear God let me get
Away
Skies dark the beaches
So crowded one did
Not know where to
Run
That was Dunkirk

E Kisby

I Signed Up

I signed up three years ago
to see the places brochures show
a cushy life, do as you please
sail the seven seas at ease.

Pompey, Pompey, three days more
Hello Darling, ship to shore
Falklands Darling, where's that place
sounds like sadness on your face.

Ship is turning stern to bow
where the hell we going now
Sorry Men our plans have changed
Falklands, there's that name again.

Action Stations, just a test
Action Stations, no more rest
Action Stations, full alert,
Don't worry Men, you'll not get hurt.

Missile, Missile, comes the cry
ten long seconds tick tock by
It whistles past I breath a sigh
Sheffield gets it, many die.

Men our Duty here is done
We've got the Argies on the run
A heroes welcome waits for you
Mum, Dad, Wife and children too

On deck waving to the crowd
Me, a Hero; makes me proud
but truth is, in reality
I was there, I had to be.
R Goodred

They Did Not Die in Vain

Mourn not for them, though they are gone;
They would not have it so.
But keep the memories always fresh,
Although the tear-drops flow.
They knew, they went, they sacrificed
Young lives for you and me,
And also for Old England,
To keep her strong and free.
Into the great unknown they sailed
With heads held proud and high.
Today we still remember them
As years go rolling by.
And now they dwell in Heaven above,
Freed from all earthly plain.
We that are left must strive to see
They did not die in vain.

R Robson

The Probationer Nurse

Oh, darling, is my cap on straight
And is my apron clean,
My stockings have no holes in them
And I look bright and keen?

You're looking just the ticket,
So svelte, my dearest Kate.
Let us go beard the Sister
And learn our daily fate.

Oh, Kate, you're sent to Theatre
With all those surgeons cool,
But I'm despatched into the sluice
And do I feel a fool!

I do not get to nurse the sick
Nor soothe the fevered brow
Of handsome, wounded officers.
That's Sister's perk, the cow.

But I am good at scrubbing baths
And making bedpans shine,
So I suppose I am some use.
Yippee, I feel just fine!

R Norton

12.8.40

'If I never live again,
This day will always be,
A rapture of my soul.
A treasured memory.
If I go down ere night,
At least this day I knew,
With all its combat wild,
In skies of azure hue.
Old Time, with cruel scythe,
Sends all memories to decay:
yet, neither Death, nor Time,
Can ever steal this day.
If I never live again ...

Sgt Pilot E Linmar (posted missing 13.8.40)

North West Frontier - 1940
(Emotion recollected in tranquillity in 1983)

The Khyber's spiky mountains
Are made of grit and rock.
It has no crystal fountains
Its wilderness to mock.

When I feel discontented
I instantly recall
How deeply I lamented
That I was there at all.

My choice, to serve my country,
Was quite correctly made;
But not for mere survival
At 120o in the shade!

Your letters did not reach me.
My cables went astray.
The bombs rained down on 'Blighty',
And I was far away.

Not all the War's privations
Were of the gastric kind.
The lack of loved relations
Was more than just a 'bind'.

No word, no touch, no kisses
For four unending years; -
The heart's starvation this is,
Not satisfied by tears.

The War has long been over
And we have long been wed,
But you are still the lover
Who followed where I led.

R Plowden

The Young The Brave
and The Strong

Hospitals .
at the ready
Medical staff
prepared
back home
everybody cared
and when
contrary to all belief
the injuries were few
we all experienced the relief
until the casualties came through
our grief was not for numbers
our loss was each precious one
someone's daughter, sister, brother
someone's father, husband, son
we shall remember them
those who helped to right a wrong
how could we ever forget
the young the brave the strong.

T Segal

Remembrance

Pale Autumn sun glints on old cross of stone,
Ranks of medalled men. Heads bowed, now grey of tone,
Comrades remembered who were once young and gay,
Who's spirits are with us on this their special day,
Remember, Remember, the hot Normandy Plains,
Burmas tangled jungle, and sudden Monsoon Rains,
Icy artic convoys, and gallant aircrews too,
and the never forgotten, glorious few,
then we sing O Lord with me abide,
and wear our scarlet poppies with pride.

K Potter

Kite-hawk Over the Desert

Part red, part brown, black-barred, and with a head
Of greyish-white, he builds his nest with sticks.
For these and other scraps, where men have bled
In desert-lands, and saints accepted kicks,
He soars beneath the blue, above the red
Of day's hot sand. The weary camel licks
Thick mud. The kite flies by the dead
Of battle, hardly hears the clicks
Of bayonet-fixing, or of metal tread
Of tank, or safety-catch. He knows our tricks
Too well. With summer's dried up river-bed
As our last refuge, in our desperate fix,
We watch him hover, scorning noon's bright sun,
And wonder if our time is nearly done.

K Parker (8th Army)

In the Silence

As you stood there in the Silence, on this bleak November day.
As the memories came aflooding. Man! What did your conscience
say?
Travelling backwards through the years, Ypres, Mons and blood
stained Flanders.
Were your thoughts on lowly privates? Did you think of great
commanders?
As you stood in dedication, as each memory took it's place.
Was there room for meditation for this mixed up human race?
Neath a million wooden crosses, men are resting, some unnamed.
Must their slaughter be forgotten? Or their dying be defamed?
Dunkirk, Arnheim, bombers, fighters. Was it ships at Matapan?
Stalingrad or Pearl Harbour? Alemein, - or Common Man?
See a child with it's father. See it laughing. See it play.
See a child without a father. What a price a child must pay.
See a lonely soldier's widow. Just suppose that she could choose.
Husband or a decoration? - Which would you prefer to lose?
The human race means not just country, nor the colour, nor the creed
Black or White, or Brown or Yellow. They all spring from human
seed.

The human race has many problems, many battles to be won.
Without the sacrifice of manhood at the altar of the gun.
Disease to conquer, oceans harnessed. Mighty deserts to be tamed.
From the highest to the lowest. Stupid man! Are you not shamed?
When shall man call each his brother? When shall man leave hate
behind?
Or will his warlike instincts smother all the good that's in mankind?
Puny man. - Forget your vanity!
Senseless man. - Restore your sanity!
In the name of stark humanity,
Man speak peace to all Mankind ...!

E Nutt

26

Desert Storm

Bombs fall from the sky with deadly power,
Relentlessly on hour by hour.
B52's drone overhead,
How many more will soon be dead.

The conflict of the Middle East,
For many years has never ceased.
Iraq, Saudi, Israel, Kuwait,
All embroiled in a war of hate.

The scuds rain down on Israel,
Patriots are fired, some will fail.
Tel Aviv, Haifa, Jerusalem,
No retaliation. Good for them.

Soldiers in the sand await,
Orders to start. What is their fate.
The airborne attack, will it win,
Or will the brave lads have to go in.

What, we say caused all this fuss,
Is it anything to do with us.
The black crude we call oil,
Is it this that brought it to the boil.

Now the oil laps around the shore,
Tons and tons. How much more.
Wildlife perish in a man made hell,
Ecological disaster Who can tell.

Bush Major, Saddam Hussein,
Are they wrong. All insane.
When the war comes to a halt,
Who's to blame, Who's at fault.

The lessons learned, will man heed,
Not while he's eaten up with greed.
Perhaps one day wars will cease,
Hopefully then there will be Peace.

Leslie Webb

Aftermath (Normandy - June 1944)

A word, a thought, will oft re-call
Scenes that in the mem'ry linger;
Traced indelibly on the mind,
'Til woken by mental finger.

A troop of tanks, still in formation,
As clear as in a painted frieze;
So very quiet, so very still,
Silhouetted against the trees.

Rememb'ring still in full detail,
The orders were to probe and feel;
'Til, just before the goal was reached,
All hell let loose it's hail of steel.

The crack of armour piercing shot:
The shattering crash of penetration:
The shower of sparks; The sheet of flame:
Blackened figures against the glow:
The slow crackling of rending steel:
The clouds of black, foul, pouring smoke:
At intervals, the vivid crimson flashes:
The violent rendering of exploding ammunition.

And then that all pervading stench,
That brings back thoughts of all the fears;
The reek of burnt-out steel and flesh
That lingers on over the years.

Those distant mem'ries linger on,
Then into distance fade again,
To stay dormant until they rise
Once more, re-called to tax the brain.

H Horsfall

Comrades

Side by side, to school each day,
More closely still on holidays.
To fight, to lark about or run.
Sharing with zest, each hour of fun.
A ball to catch, a game to win.
A book to read, a hiding earned.
So many things, we knew as boys,
The depth of comradeship, we learned.

The years roll on. time seems to fly.
We've grown up fast have you and I.
At work we sweat, wear and hide.
From early dawn, to eventide
We fall in love, and chase the girls.
So many that post memory whirls.
Yet once, when each finds his ideal,
Best man to each with eager zeal.
A foursome now, yet comrades still.

All goes well, 'til comes the call,
When England's backs are to the wall.
Together still, with manly pride,
We join the ranks, still side by side.
Through desert's heat and battles roar,
We sweat and swear and pray with awe.
so much to do, we know the fear,
Of hanging on, with death too near.
Yet how it helps when comrades share.

At last it ends, the battles won.
A new world is promised later on.
We find our homes are sweet and fair,
Compared with all the hell out there.
We settle down, to work and play,
To make the most of each new day.
With children's voices in our ears,
Drowning all those, now past fears,
As comrades still, we face the years.

G F Allen (Gunner - Royal Artillery)

Alamein Revisited

There's a sense of desolation... there's a ghostly moon on high,
and the silver sands are silent... as a wind goes whisp'ring by,
There's a feeling of great sadness... with the shadows dark and deep,
and the silver sands are murmering... as tho' wakening from their
sleep.
They seem to whisper secrets of those days so long ago,
when the sands were red with life blood... and the moon... a crimson
glow.
There's a phantom bugler sounding reville... loud and clear,
and an army stirs and wakens... as the fateful hour draws near,
and our memories are awakening as we hear that trumpet blast...
of dust... and dirt... and danger... of the dim and distant past.
There's the sound of footsteps marching... as they marched there
once before
and the ghosts of comrades mingle... as they gather there once more.
There are small... white crosses gleaming... in the cold light of the
moon,
like silent mute reminders of a life... cut down too soon.
And they seem to ask a question... in a silent whispering pause...
Will you who pass forget us... or our brave and valiant cause?
Back comes our answer swiftly... triumphant... loud... and clear...
No... we can never forget you... or the cause you held so dear,
as long as the sands shall whisper... and the years roll round again,
we will remember... comrades... comrades of Alamein.

Angus Willis

Nineteen Sixteen Remembered

I remember this place, when I was here last
That was, oh, so many, many years past,
So long ago, yet I remember it well
When these green fields were the very pastures of hell!

We were sent up as part of the great attack,
Thousands set out, only hundreds came back!
'So great are our numbers, it will be easy,' they said,
But by nightfall great numbers of our lads lay dead.

Husbands and fathers, brothers and sons
All fell prey to the insatiable guns.
Companies, battalions, wiped out to a man,
All in pursuit of some master plan.

We fought like tigers to gain a few yards of mud,
Every yard gained was paid for in blood.
Many men died without knowing why,
But whatever the reason, the price was too high!

But I'm glad that I came, to see just once more
This place I remember from that long ago war,
To call into mind, Joe, Harry and Tom,
My pals who lie somewhere, here on the Somme.

W Green

Early Closing

You were drafted,
Windswept
Like the leaves
That Autumn early closing day
Their colour matched
Your uniforms.
Whilst champions
Drove liberating tanks
You rode your bike
In unheroic Lancs.
With youthful haste
The unfamiliar sign was passed
The driver's instantaneous prayer.
A cry for Mom,
But soon the early closing
Calm returns.
And later,
Stinted wartime news
'US Soldier's Accidental Death'
They gave no name.
Even days have names;
'Remembrance'
'Early Closing'

Norman Hadland

The Bombing of Deal Barracks - 1989

The Royal Marine.
'Per Mare, Per Terram'.
In times of strife, all kinds of wars
To foreign lands or lonely shores
By land, by sea and even air
The Royal Marine goes anywhere.
But these were young musicians, whose music filled the air
Dear God above, please let them know that we really care
Our hearts are full of grief and sorrow
For those young men there's no tomorrow
With these few thoughts and silent prayer
Take them in thy loving care.

Jackie Dray

Dark Waters

In dark waters he lay
Lost in the depths of Neptunes land
One more sailor in death: in this savage bay.
Never more to feel the comfort of a mothers hand.
Nor the sweet kiss and caress of a lover.
The life cut short by smothering water.
Deep he lay no knowledge of night or day.
No runs ashore in beaming happy band.
This the sailors last visit to a foreign land.
Here no sights to see no market in which to barter.
Only dark waters for now and ever after.

E C Inkpen

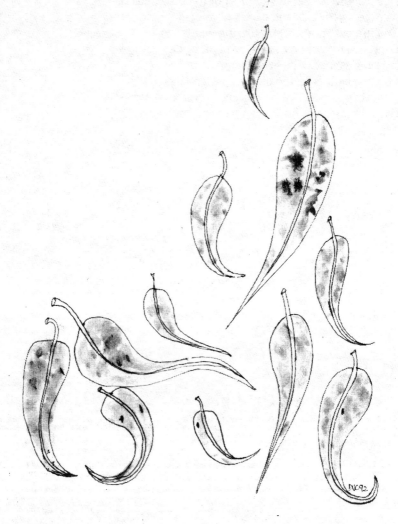

The Falling Leaves

'Catch the falling leaves,' said he,
'And our fortunes we'll be told'.
So we caught the falling leaves,
Red and yellow, green and gold.

Red for danger - yes that's true;
His soldier's beret what that Hue.
Yellow was his curly hair
That framed the face I thought so fair.

Green the grass that covers his grave
My soldier son; who was so brave.
Gold I'd give to hear again
His footsteps echoing in the lane.

No more we'll walk beneath the trees
And catch the falling Autumn leaves
No more our fortunes we'll be told
Red and Yellow, Green and Gold.

M Vosper

Remember the Young Men

As I return from the cenotaph I know they'll be waiting
they'll be there with their mocking and infantile baiting.
Throw us your buttonhole old man they cry,
but I ignore them walk by them with steel in my eye,
still I look at gnarled hands as tough as old leather
a face grined and wrinkled by inclement weather
and at hair now sprinkled and powdered with grey.
But my mind is still young, so I return to that day
to that time in Korea with Winters so mean,
They say it was nothing to the wars that have been,
oh yes you can tell me I know its been spoken.
But I'll show you the ricefield where bodies lay broken
and I'll tell of a comrade whose just passed away
a hero forgotten unremembered today.
But I fought by his side for each one of you
and I remember his courage and bravery too
so don't scorn me for wearing this poppy with pride
remember the young men when for all of us died.

J B Watkinson

Untitled

The soldiers on either side,
are crucified.
So why does Jesus stand
in no mans land?

Sydney R Undrell

The 14th Army

The forgotten army they were called,
And still are known as such.
But none of us should 'ere forget
Those to whom we owe so much.
They left their homes and loved ones
For far and distant shores.
To fight a foe they did not know,
In the bloodiest of wars.
Through the heat, the mud, the jungle
The monsoons, and the flies,
Though weary to their very soul,
With tired red rimmed eyes
They battled on from day to day,
A bit of ground to gain,
And many were the wounded, and many more, the slain
They buried comrades where they fell,
With hardly time to pray.
Then left them in Gods keeping,
And returned into the fray.
No, let us not forget them, those men from near and far
Now on their chests, a medal rests,
It's called the 'Burma Star'
And out there in Kohima
A stone there stands, away
On it these words are written
'When you go home, tell them of us, and say,
'For your 'tomorrows'
We gave our 'today'

D Moore

The Italian Chapel, Orkney

The little Italian chapel,
The painting of the White Dove.
A shrine to the human spirit,
A symbol of faith and love.

A triumph over adversity,
Loneliness and defeat,
Echoing in it's silence
The tramp of prisoner's feet.

Fashioned in iron and concrete,
Embellished with loving care,
A glorious inspiration
For all who enter there.

*Note: This chapel was erected by Italian prisoners of war who were
interned in Camp 60 on the tiny island of Lamb Holm, Orkney in the
1940's. A corrugated-iron Nissen hut was transformed into a unique
and beautiful little chapel. It was constructed out of waste materials
and the interior is adorned with exquisite freehand paintings.*

Christine Oddy

Merseyside At War

Memories over half a century old
Of bombing so extensive
Still referred to as the May Blitz.
Part of Goering's 'Port Offensive.'

Of the maternity ward at Mill Road
Where, a deadly accurate bomb
Killed all the mothers except two
All the babies except one.

Of a family who lost nine relatives
And were bombed out from their house
Returned to search the wreckage
To save a precious pan of scouse.

Of that lovely bright May morning
With the trees all draped in white
With gun cotton from the ammo train
Which had been exploding through the night

Memories also come flooding back
To the horror of Durning Road
Where Luftflotten one and two
Rained down its deadly load.

One hundred and sixty six people died
In that ill fated Edge Hill School
Which was chosen as a target
In the Port of Liverpool

For those many air raid victims
Hundreds unidentified
There is a much vandalized Blitz memorial
A common grave for all who died.

Alex S Edwards

Wear Your Poppy with Pride
Why?

We do not celebrate or commemorate wars.
Only those who have suffered the loss, grief, parting and pain
truly understand the horrors such conflicts bring.

We do not live in Utopia or the Garden of Eden but -
we have the freedom of speech, choice, religion and travel.
These freedoms are denied to too many people on our planet
and are envied. There has been and will be people
who wish to take them away from us.

The suffering borne by past and present generations is of those
who have fought and guarded these freedoms for us to enjoy.
You wear your poppy to show that you are a caring
civilised person who appreciates what ever little you have and
has been bequeathed to you
So go thy why in peace.

As a young soldier wrote in world war one
'I hope those at home will not betray our trust in them.'

Will you?

God Bless

R Ewen

Untitled

I sometimes wonder if the end is near or far away,
Or is it just a passing thought I'm thinking of today,
Four years we have been fighting for life and British soil.
What will be the end of all the sweating, blood and toil?
Will this world of ours be giving credit due,
To all the tired people and start itself anew.
Or will it be a place of woe, starvation and of tears.
And start itself another war in ten or twenty years!
Many men must think as I, as did our fathers years gone by.
When out in France on Flanders Plains
Their losses were the Germans gains
But on they fought one thing in view
They fought to make a world anew
And when the final battles came
Backs to the wall they won the game.
Oh world I dread of such a mess
That kids today in school boy dress
Shall fight one day for what is right
We just don't know. they might, they might.

John Thomas Preston Keeling

The RAF Flying Instructor

'What did you do in the war Daddie?' 'Taught people to fly Laddie'
'Like a teacher in the class?' 'No! In a Tiger on the grass'
A Tiger Moth, a little plane, a trainer plus - of wartime fame
As tough as nails and rugged too. Lets fly away into the blue
Take off now and then we climb. Then straight and level for a time,
Turns, rate one, both left and right, Thro' a cloud, no sense of height,
Stalls and spins and then recover, loop the loop and then another.
Time now then to go back home. Where? Oh where's the aerodrome?
Instructor knows, it's soon in sight. left on circuit, never right.
Downwind leg now, level flight. Left-hand turn to crosswind leg,
Now throttle back and into glide. Engine quiet - oh, what a ride!
Gliding turn now - not too fast. Boundary hedges we soon pass,
All clear ahead, stick gently back. Ground rushes by - we're on the
grass!
So now we're down and yet no fright. We've done it. Yes. Your fine
first flight
Later on, days more tuition. First solo flight your full fruition.

'What did you do in the war Daddie?' 'Taught people to fly Laddie
We turned up trumps - spins and stalls and 'Circuits and Bumps'

Circuits and Bumps - RAF slang for Take off and Landing. The most
difficult part of training for pupil pilots

Dave Crook

Ballad of a Soldier

From the peace of a quiet garden
To another land far away
I think of a promise I gave you
That last late Autumn day

I'll be home by early April
When the daffodils are blooming
And the blossom trees have flowers
Do not think I have forgotten
That faded dream of ours

My friends are resting in the twilight
Just quietly their voices flow
Last night I heard one singing
A song which echoes thoughts I know

If I'm not home before November
When the summer is forgotten
And the roses have declined
Just remember that first Springtime
We walked together side by side

Pauline Kavanagh

Premonition in Burma

We heard you sing the songs of France
In the mess at midnight,
While the parched earth bathed her burning face
Under the starlight.

The tent was filled with memories
As your fingers strayed
Over the strings of the guitar,
So easily you played.

Next day we stood beside your grave
Carved in the mountain side,
Remembering the liberty
For which you died.

The trumpet sounded and the fire
Of rifles smote the air.
(How fearlessly a man last night
Of death became aware).

Randle Manwaring

Who was to Blame for it all?

Singapore we held no more
Our struggle was in vain,
We had the guns, we had the men
But not a single plane.

The battle raged from left to right,
We were in a bloody plight
Bombed and shelled both day and night
But still our planes were not in sight.

Our orders were to hold our ground
Although our comrades lay dead around.
For days no rest, no sleep at night
But still our lads were full of fight.

Singapore was all aglow
Our food supply was running low
Hour by hour we held our ground
Waiting for that droning sound.

Spitfires and Hurricans we saw no more
Our water supply, it flowed no more
For water and planes our choice was first
But the sight of our planes would quench our thirst

The Nippon forces were advancing fast
To fight the dive bombers was too great a task
Dug-outs and shell holes we made our homes
To advance was suicide, which made the boys moan.

The odds were too great
We knew not our fate
For Singapore we knew must fall
But, 'Who was to blame for it all'?

(ex W.R.E.N. and wife of Ex 2nd Bn Cambridgeshire Reg
                                    F.E.P.O.W.)

M J Howes

Memories

The skylark above the meadow
soars,
Scattered poppies avoid the reapers blade,
and Tommy remembers comrades beneath
the greensward, well laid.

S Shakespeare (R.A.S.C.)

By the Banks of the Nile: 1942

A year is dead - a year is born
The Nile flows on in silent scorn
The banks which yielded fertile minds
Have buried far more varied kinds.

The fools who sought to rule the earth
Rewarded hate, to death gave birth
The wiser fools who sought the cause
Have paused to think - and thought to pause.

The silvery line of truth still flows
By-passing history's sick side-shows.
A cold wet tomb to wasted youth
A monument of mirrored truth.

It flows on still though sands are red.
The water flows as the year falls dead.
It flows past rulers long asleep
Who snarled like wolves and yet proved sheep.

Those aspirants for such power and fame
Ascended in fire, descended in flame.
Our prophets saw beyond these mists
Swim on with life, were realists.

So come New Year, Life's river swells
The Reich is sick. Ring out the bells!
With Time's strong stroke cross-currents we'll breast.
With Life we flow where others jest.

Stanley S Segal

The Women of the 40's

Leaving their homes was not easy you know, leaving their homes
                                        and preparing to go,
Into the W.A.A.F. and leaving behind their colleagues, their pals and
                                        their friendships that bind,
Leaving behind the place where they worked so long, leaving their
                                        post and the cities dense throng,
Taking their chances along with the rest, risking their lives with a
                                        song and a jest,
One day in civvies and all dressed for the town, the next day in blue
                                        but never a frown,
One day on mufti awaiting news, the next day in tunics and thick Air
                                        Force shoes,
Thousands of them gave up their jobs, and the heart of this country
                                        still pulses and throbs,
Because of these girls that answered the call, wherever they are now,
Good luck to them all.

L K Newling

Peace

And England, while rejoicing, wept;
The sky, that shielded those who slept,
Was still. Peace reigned supreme -
Britannia dreamed her quiet dream....

Marian Fairchild

I Remember...

As a school boy of ten in '38
the rumblings of war threatening Europe's fate
Mr Chamberlain's trip across the Rhine
and his proclamation 'peace in our time'

The solemn announcement in '39
we're at war with Germany, for a second time
the military call-up of 'young faces' then
and civilians organised for war, yet again

The issue of gas masks and ration books new
identity cards and the blackout too
Auxiliary services, armed forces and all
defending our shores from the enemies call.

Children evacuated by train, boat and bus
to safe destinations with minimum fuss
name labels attached, gas masks in tow
to far away places, off they did go

Bombs and fires, the sirens wailed
shelters cold, but spirits prevailed
sleep was hard through the night
but morning came and on with the fight

Churchill's speeches to the nation at war
urging us forward to the victory he saw
from 'we'll never surrender' in '40, so clear
to 'war's over - we've won' in '45, that year

For six long years we had fought the fight
now bells rang clear and we could see the light
thanksgiving services throughout the lands
victory parades, marches and bands

Children's street parties, laughter and tear
as the forces came home to their loved one's so dear.

Bernard East

Chindit

Have you ever seen a column march away,
And you left lying, too damned sick to care?
Have you ever watched the night crawl into day
With red-rimmed eyes that are too tired to stare?
Have you ever bled beside a jungle trace
In thick brown mud like coagulating stew?
Have you ever counted leeches loping back
Along the trail of sweat that leads to you?
Have you ever heard your pals shout 'cheerio',
Knowing that this is no 'Auf wiedersehn'?
Have you ever prayed, alone, for help although
The stench of mules has vanished in the rain?
Have you ever thought 'what a bloody way to die!',
Left in the tree-roots, rotting, there to stay?
God, I remember last poignant 'Goodbye';
I was one of the men that marched away.

K N Batley

PDC92

60

This Peace Atomic

All this, the aftermath;
The end of strife, of blood and sweat, the turning
off the narrow way where devils met,
the loathsome, treacherous path of war.

All this, the end;
This seething, boiling caldron which is the world.
Its nations banners defiant on high unfurled,
flaunting their triumphs unheeded over all.

All this, the aftermath;
The sinister, darkening plume of dust and smoke,
the ages blasted, the might roar or promise spoke -
Perchance this is The End.

R Greaves

Future Generations

Silent were the hedgerows,
Silent were the fields
The hillsides and the valleys;
We only hear the streams.

Children in the distance
Churchbells are muffled there;
We all stood there defiant,
We stood there and we dared.

With pride we can remember,
When England stood alone;
We may have saved all Europe,
We saved our island home.

Memories like burnt embers
Are fading fast away;
But we, who still remember,
Can stand with pride and say

Those children in the distance
Are playing there today;
In hedgerows birds are nesting,
The fields have new mown hay.

The streams we still hear running,
Hillsides with morning dew,
The valleys are now singing,
Churchbells are ringing true.

We all stood so defiant;
Our thanks we gave in prayer,
That England is still England
Because we stood and dared.

Peace unite the nations;
We ask for this in prayer
For future generations,
May peace be everywhere.

Alwyn Scammells

The Death of Dresden (Feb 14th 1945)

Dresden, fairest city in the land,
Unmet with hostile vehemence of might,
In hours reduced to ashes by the hand
That merely pressed a button in the night.

How impersonal this - a finger's touch
To kill a hundred thousand folk
Removing centuries of history much
As the button-pusher tells a joke.

William Hoare

On Tap

'Shortage of water', I hear you say,
Yet you go for a beer at the end of the day
To despise old folk who talk about war
Because - 'everyone knows there won't be any more'.
'Comradeship', you say that's all crap.
Yet they work at it whilst you just yap.
'Gutless old has-beens who just talk wet -'?
You wanna bet 'flower' -
You wanna bet?

Charles White R.A.F.A.

The Somme

There was a sense of desolation there
Although we toured the district at our ease;
I think it was the lasting lack of trees
That made the rolling pastureland seem bare,
The thought that trees had once grown freely where
The stunned and staggered eye now merely sees
A verdant grassland laced with cemeteries
And villages replete with peaceful air.
A little over sixty years ago
Men writhed and wrangled with the common foe,
And fought to gain an extra yard of mud
And paid the price in unrelenting blood ---
My uncle, poets, heroes, poor men died,
And we sat brooding at their cold grave side.

Dick Hedger

Bomber Command

They came from far and wide
young! and rearing to help the
cause, knowing no danger! they
had youth! but soon became
weary and old!
But no regrets as they had come
and did the job of helping
the cause, of freedom.

Nora Kemp Richmond W.A.A.F., Bomber Command

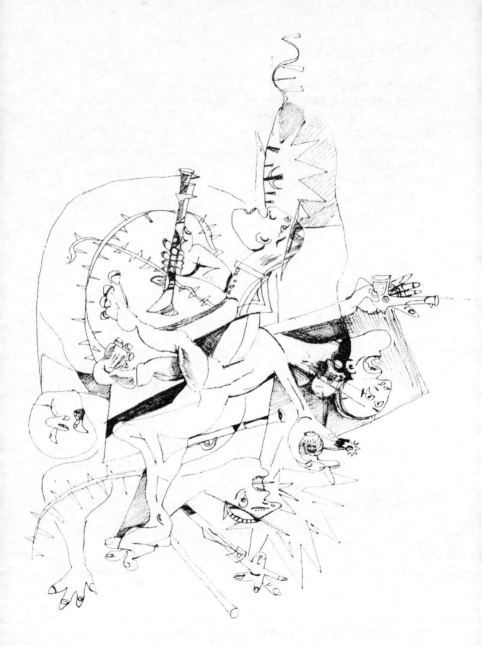

France September - 1916 Guillemont

They lie there with their mouths agape.
Echoes of their shouts not long gone.,
Tossed about like broken rag dolls,
Surrounded by mists in muddy knolls.

They are all blind now and cannot see,
My mates like statues lying there,
A thousand scarecrows in a foreign field
The only thing they scare is me.

Stan Yates

22nd January 1945

The rumours for once were accurate,
the rumours for once were right,
and we were leaving Lamsdorf,
on a bitter January night.
On uneven snow that was frozen,
on ice that tore muscle roots,
some murmured and cursed but were grateful
that at least they had decent boots.
Some soon tired of the burden
of carrying their Stalag loot,
and dropped their treasured belongings
not caring or giving a hoot.
'Keep right' and 'hurry' were the orders,
And curses replied all along,
when from the front of the column
some voices were heard in song.
'Tipperary' and 'Pack up your Troubles'
among the ranks were sung,
but soon the cold and the effort
took its toll and silence hung.
At last there's a 'halt', and we huddled,
From hand to hand fag ends glow,
When finished they're quickly extinguished
in the hard and the frozen snow.
Late in the hours of that evening
in the sheds and barns bodies lay,
so weary and aching and frozen
that they don't want to see the next day.
Some don't; and are left there forever
and as the march went along,
others lay down for the last time
and the column cared not for a song.

Peter Skinner

Market Garden

My eyes fill with tears,
As I gaze at the summer sky.
The scudding clouds and birds
Are natures gift to the living.
No more do man made birds
With lethal loads soar overhead
And all around our glorious dead
The Village is quiet now
A haven in peaceful countryside
Not as on those awful days
When the streets were thronged
By men in brown and grey
Much determined the honour of
His country would not fail
From city and town they had come
Some young. Others in their prime
And on the side
The reaper called his time
Now they rest
But they have won immortal fame
Will Oosterbake
Be just another name.

A Jones

Return from Atlantic Patrol

They came back to base in the darkness
Returned from an ocean wide
They knew of the presence of death
But they had no fear to hide
For their duty demands that they face it
They know life leads but to the grave
They'll give all they have for their country
So honour the men who are brave

They saw the dim glinting lanterns
Laid out that they might alight
They approached towards comfort and safety
Finished with flying that night .
But alas, a few moments later
The aircraft plunged into the sea
Their cries rang into the darkness
As their limbs they struggled to free.

The aircraft broke in a moment
That moment meant life for a few
But 'twas not enough for six others
And what could their comrades do?

So they went to join their companions
On the bed of the Forth of Lorne
They're safe from the perils of flying
Secure from all mortal storm

They'll be joining up with a Squadron
Whose duties are not of this earth
They'll be working well for that Squadron
Awaiting their day of rebirth.
For now those Sunderland aircraft
Two in number under the sea
Enough to start a new Squadron
And fly in spirit with me.

They gave their lives for their country
No nobler deed than this
We honour the cause that they died for
May they all rest in perfect peace

Wing Cdr Derek Martin OBE BSc

Song of Maymyo

Secluded in a mountain range...
In rural majesty -
There lies a land I once surveyed...
Two thousand feet above the sea,

... a land once mentioned in the Psalms...
Where living water flowed,
And lakes so crystal clear, I swear
God's purpose plainly showed...
... for there He took me by the hand
And showed me many fruits -
That grew beside the mountain streams
Amid the tender bamboo shoots...

I sipped the water from the stream
And felt my pulses race -
My very soul became refreshed
Whilst in His sweet embrace...

I stood beneath a sapphire sky -
And gloried in His touch...
And to this day, no memory
Can stir my heart so much...!

Secluded in a mountain range...
There is a land I know -
A land where I once saw the light...
And heard the Song of Maymyo...!

(Burma 1945)

Russell Humphrey

74

Remembrance

Faintly hear them marching, faintly hear them sing,
·Those who fought for us, and freedom, remembering,
For they never alter, and they will not age,
Remember those who helped us win our heritage.

Dead soldiers line the street of memory,
Salute the brave ones, who set us free;
Comrades, arm in arm they stand,
As if waiting for that final command.

Airforce and Navy, side by side,
Women too, who helped the war subside,
Who won the war, and lost their fight
To reap rewards, which was their right.

Look back and remember the brave,
Call back the years, when they forgave
The blunders others refuse to admit;
Oh conscience, if you could only submit.

William Nichol

RDC 92

76

Private Mason's War

Your war was no bunch of roses, was it mate?
Only a bloody awful mess of stinking mud, pain, cold and hollow
cheerfulness.
Young, eager lives snuffed like spent lucifers.
Battle colours mangled with bright hopes into the crawling slime -
And over all, the terrible earnestness,
The do-or-die, scared as hell, blind gallantry
That created heroes - and casualty lists!
Still, there might well have been more spontaneity,
More earthy solace in your mud and blood and onion flavoured tea
Than in the slick, push-button annihilation
Planned for our kids by some cold-eyed fool in a laboratory.
Beyond the agony and horror of your dug-out
There seemed to be some kind of future - even if it was an illusion.
Next time the boys will be going home to total extinction.

Joan B Howes

Together Yet Apart

Yesterday when we were together you by chance said to me
That now that bereavement has come to you, you can no longer see
The sense of all this birth and death and why it had to be
Could we not live for ever and grow old eternally?

Today as you sit thinking of all that has come and gone,
The good times spent together, now that you're sadly alone,
You cannot see the point of getting up each day,
Your heart seems so very laden, is this the price you must pay?

Tomorrow when you have dried your tears, because time will heal,
                                                'tis said
Your heart has now a vacant place, what future looms ahead?
Your loved one would not wish you to sit and grieve all day
But try to find a purpose in life: you know it's the only way.

Next year as you look backwards at what happened yesterday
Your loved one will be close to you, in yet another year you'll say
That time had healed the broken heart, doubtful though now it seems
The fleeting years will bring you hope, together yet apart.

What of your future as you tread the path of life each day?
Finding new interest and work wherever your feet may stray.
You know it will lead to sweet memories tho' some could be sombre
                                                and gray
Time is kind, never be in doubt, as you travel along life's way.

Olive Willingale

The Last Op

A solemn comradeship embraces
The tense white arc of youthful faces
And many a mother's cherished son
Goes forth once more to fight the Hun

Swift fall the shades of purple night
Whilst sitting out around the kite
A deathlike silence greets the ear
Each thinks of home and loved ones dear

An engine starts with shattering roar
Then two and three and dozens more
We taxi out into the line
Each with a date across the Rhine

Control looms up from out the gloom
Our engines wake with mighty boom
Then down the runway swift we go
And soon the airfield lies below

The aircraft's nose is pointing east
We're heading out to kill the beast
The English coastline falls away
We'll meet dear land another day

We sight the target all aflame
There's bags of flack the Bosch is game
A kite goes down like falling leaf
And seven homes are marred with grief

'Bombs gone' we weave like mad to fool
The lurking Jerry fighter school
We break away and homeward bound
Our eardrums ache with endless sound

England lies once more ahead
'My God' I'm tired let's get to bed
To feel firm ground beneath our feet
Once more my friend is very sweet

W S Boulter

Malaya 1950

Breaking the jungle silence, the shuffle and muffled tramp,
The whispered curse, the stifled cough of a company breaking camp,
The officer gives his orders by the light of a hurricane lamp:
'Terrorists are reported in a village two miles ahead,
Twenty or thirty in number, or so the informer said.
The company is to attack at dawn and get them, alive or dead;
A platoon to each flank, to surround them, with fire from left and
right,
The remainder advance in the centre and lie close up, out of sight,
To close for the kill with the bayonet - the attack will begin at first
light.'
Dawn - and the troops in position - exactly according to plan,
A whistle, the rattle of Bren guns, the assault troops advance as one
man
Through a scattered volley fired by the terrorist band as they ran.
'Own casualties - two killed, three wounded; enemy casualties - *nil* -'
March back and wait for the next report - (we're getting to know the
drill!)
'Terrorist band reported - on the other side of the hill!'

Lieut Col R A A Dawes MC

Tread Softly

Tread softly as you walk the sunken path.
Tread softly, or you'll miss the nervous laugh.
Quietly they call, then sharply cry,
As bullets whine, and young men slump and die.

Tread softly, friends are all around,
Snugly they lie beneath the mossy ground.
You'll catch a whiff of woodbine on the air
But do not strain your eyes, they're everywhere.

They quietly watch, as you go by
And think, as you are now, so once was I.
They stay, you leave, and can return,
It's that which makes them sadly yearn,

Tread softly then, and creep away.

Lieut Col Dennis Hampton Jeffery

Requiem to a Pair of Boots
(on an Unknown Soldier in the retreat from Kuwait -
February 1st 1991)

Feet splayed outwards
soles upwards - a pair of boots
extends beyond blanketed body,
Concealing identity - one of thousands
of corpses of men and machines
littering the road to Baghdad
in the retreat from Kuwait.

Was he young, was he old?
Kurd or Iraqi?
Conscript or seasoned veteran?

Did he become bolder by experience -
had he raped, fired the flames that set
oil tanks ablaze? Released the flow
that engulfed comorants far away -
blackening sands of shores
he would never see?

Had he been homesick with no stomach
for war? Envious of others' property
he saw in the looting - here's a toy
for his child, perfume for his wife,
possessions beyond his purse?

We shall never know... we shall never know.

Only his boots cry out to the passing
sweep of a camera's eye. His contribution
to questions unanswered.

Arda Lacey

Tranquillity

The beautifully coloured heathers,
A rainbow of falling leaves,
Red berry, and blossomed trees.
The gentle breeze of Autumn,
Whispering voices, and laughter,
Drifting through the trees.

With swallows gliding through the air,
Thistle seeds, ascending everywhere,
Like parachutes floating to the ground.
An invasion of joking, and laughter,
That is how it sounds.
It was a joyful, exquisite treat.

An instant thought of Oosterbeek.
Had my comrades come from there?
Just a short flip away,
To this activity by day.
At sunset they could then return,
To rest among the trees, and stones.

I'm pleased I found their little game,
They have not grown old, or weary,
Like us that had survived the fray,
They are happy and contented.
Waiting for their loved one's,
To join them once again.

I'm so glad to be back again,
To share this happy daydream,
I feel contented in my mind,
To think and feel what I have seen,
This beauty, and tranquillity,
Nearby Arnhem, Airborne Cemetery.
Norrie Hill 3rd Parachute Battalion

The Poppy that is Red

Who are you?
You!... Who campaign for world peace
Concocted white poppies as a symbol of peace,
Who are you to say *we* glorify war?
Just because it's the red poppy we wore?
We... The men who wear the poppy that's red
We... The men who weep for our glorious dead
We... The men who watched our comrades die,
We are the men who fought death in the sky,
We men stormed the Normandy beaches
We are the men who sailed the Western reaches.
What do you know of the horrors of war,
Of the stink and the terror and the abundance of gore?
But *we*... the men who faced flying steel,
We... the men who knew fear that was real
We the men who shed precious blood,
We the men who lived in the shit and the mud...
We know!
We who faced death at each dawn
We the men whose flesh has been torn.
We men who survived a living hell,
We the comrades of those who fell,
How dare you
Accuse us of glorifying wars,
When our minds and our bodies still carry the scars
So... go ahead continue your fight,
But bury your poppy that is coloured white!
And leave us our poppy of crimson red...
For this is how we remember... *our glorious dead!*

Bill Ridley 9th D.L.I.

85

BRITONS

"WANTS **YOU**

JOIN YOUR COUNTRY'S ARMY!

GOD SAVE THE KING

The Years Between

Dedicated to my aunt, Miss Eva Cassandra Groves (1895 - 1990) and
her friend, Robert O'Neill, who died in the First World War.

'Kitchener calls me, Eva', you said,
'To serve both King and Country.'
And so you went to join the dead,
My valiant Robert, from me.

All I had left of you, my love,
I placed above my bed.
And so you watched me from above,
And your youthful radiance shed.

Smiling, in field grey uniform,
You have watched through aging years.
And I have grieved for those unborn
That I might have had of yours.

Each year I have placed a poppy
In the frame around your head,
'Til Flanders field, it seemed to me,
Is there shown, where your blood was shed.

Death's not the only cost of war,
But the loved ones left behind
With repeated pain of mem'ries that score
The scars on heart and mind.

Alone, unwed, I struggle on,
And time goes flying by.
Ninety-five years, in all, have gone.
Sight, strength, gone too. 'Tis time to die.

'Bob called, she went', they'll say of me,
'They loved both true and strong.
And now at last in Heaven they be,
And everlasting love their song.'

Alan James Kinsman

Tears for Yesterday

It is mother who again has come
To put a Poppy Cross upon your grave.
It says upon your headstone
That it was nineteen forty-four, that
You and many more did drop from the skies
That early September morn'
In to a place named Arnhem.
For a week you fought brave and true
But in the end you died that day,
At a bridge too far.
I wonder did you know the twins buried
on your left, or maybe the boy who
Won the Military medal who lies
on your right, could he have
been your mate
I have worried son, of who would put
The Poppy Cross upon your grave, as I am old
And time is short, but I need not fear,
For the Dutch good people that they are
Will never let you lads be forgotten.
Each year their children come,
With flowers by the armful, and you my son
Have flowers every Autumn put upon your grave.
Let me say my last farewell to you and all.
Who will forever lie in Oosterbeek.
Before I return to Cornwall, I have one more
Poppy Cross to put upon a grave.
This time in France
It's for your brother Tom who lies in Normandy.

Joan Hewitt

Weathered Weeds

Florence, Flo or Florrie, she never minded which,
Would often pause to have a chat with God.
She'd say, 'Dear Lord and master, you know that I'm not rich,
Which comes of being left upon me tod.

Old nasty took my Albert, it went against the grain,
Fate most unkind, the war was nearly won,
He'd seen it all at Dunkirk, Tobruk and Alamein,
In foreign field he lies now, 'neath a stone.

To be alone, confronted, each day with vacant chair,
Has been my lot for more than forty years.
I've felt, apart from you Lord, that no one seemed to care,
So tried to keep a private place for tears.

But now I've seen his grave Lord, and much to my surprise,
With reverence it's tended: such largesse -
From folk who never knew him, the colour of his eyes,
His voice, his smile, his grace and tenderness.

I know I've been a pain, Lord, to grouchiness I own,
To 'Jeremiaditis' much akin,
But now my heart is lighter, such peace I had not known,
It washed away the bitterness within.

So this year for the first time, I will not hide away,
Will join with countless others who give pause
To bow their heads together and in silence pray
To honour those who fell in two great wars.'

Howard Cooke

1943

At eighty, an old, old man, cutting the hedge with a sickle
It touched something and he was blasted - 'was this his war?'

They called it a Butterfly Bomb, but a butterfly is beautiful
This thing hung like a devil, waiting to kill.

We roared down the road to the crossing - a little crowd waited
                                                        nearby
'Come on man, help with this stretcher' - they looked the other way.

Struggled with our human burden - the birds were singing once more
We were leaving this scene of carnage - nearly left his leg.

Shut the doors, start her up, into gear - get to Norwich as quickly as
                                                        you can
Eyes alert, watch the road, forget the sight, five miles to go.

A tap on the communicating window, slide it along - a voice is heard
No rush, take it easy - he's dead. Killed by a butterfly.

Winifred Jones

Untitled

You do not see as here we stand
to honour you in a distant land.
You did us proud that day in *May*,
and now you watch o'er *'Suda Bay'*
You do not hear the prayers we say,
on another day, in another *May*.
Our thoughts and feelings are always here.
We'll meet again at the last *'all-clear'*.

Reg Spurr 2nd Battalion York and Lancaster Regiment

Hunter Killer

Sleek and silent, steel encased,
Beneath the rolling main,
The U-boat crew, excited, faced
The chance to kill again.

But suddenly from out the gloom,
A grey destroyers bow,
Flying depth charge, rising plume,
Despairing dive, explosion loud.

The first was close, the next a hit,
The shattered boat sank fast,
Leaking badly, black as pitch,
And choking phosgene gas.

Desperate tries to right the trim,
As creaking pipework gave,
Screams of panic, faces grim,
A mile-deep watery grave.

Another battle twixt the brave,
Another, yet another.
Eternal Father, strong to save,
Why do men destroy each other?

C H Stannard

The Evacuee

With a label on my blazer
And a suitcase in my hand,
My gas mask slung across me,
Very frightened here I stand.

I can hear some children crying,
Others laughing, but not I,
For I'm waiting very quietly,
And feeling small and shy.

We've travelled on a chugging train,
We've travelled on a bus,
And now we're lined up in the street,
And told we musn't fuss.

And the teachers study names on lists,
And knock upon each door,
'Did you say you'd have one little girl?'
And 'Could you have one more?'

I haven't got a sister,
And I haven't got a brother,
And that is why they take me out
The first of any other.

But at teatime Billy Brown's still there,
The twins are at his side,
They've got very dirty faces,
Where the tears have streaked and dried.

And I have the strangest feeling,
When I'm grown up, I'll remember,
This year of 1939,
The sad month of September.

And I'll think about the night-time,
When my Mum was far away,
And hope that other children,
Never know so long a day.

Shirley Tomlinson

Twenty-Second Birthday - France 1940

Twenty-two years ago my mother lay
Racked in travail and I first saw the light -
First looked with unknowing eyes on day
(Far better to have clung to night).

Twenty-two years ago my father lay
In Flanders mud, beneath a shell-stripped tree -
Coughing his only life away
To make a better world for me.

Twenty-two years, so short a time, and I
Shot through the belly, writhe upon the brink.
I can't help laughing, even as I die -
It's rather funny, don't you think?

Father Peter Fenwick MBE, TD

Futile War

When we were young we had a war
To give this world true peace,
As we've grown old it seems to me
That wars will never cease.
It's now upon our doorstep
In each part of our land,
Why is it that our leaders
Still fail to understand.

The sorrow that is in my heart
When someone's hurt or killed,
Bring out the thoughts within my mind -
More lives are unfulfilled.
But what is worse I must confess
And see it more and more,
The workers are the ones that kill
Each other by the score.

Surely now we've got to find
A way to stop it all,
For land and power can never be
The workers' only goal.
Most of us just like to work
And be at peace with others.
Let's make the world a safer place
For children and their mothers.

J Lever

Arnott's Issue Army Fighting Biscuits

'We don't want bacon, kidney, eggs
We don't want any grill,
We don't want beans on toast
Because they'd only make us ill'

'Cold pickled pork would make us belch,
And so would brawn or brisket,
But send us please occasionally,
A good old *Arnott's* biscuit'.

(Written in a Japanese POW Camp in Palembang, Sumatra, when on
starvation rations.)

Anonymous

Where Now

Where are they now
The Dusty Miller's, Chalky White's and Dolly Gray's,
Those good companions
Of our war torn days,
Where is the New Jerusalem
For which we fought,
The rainbow that we chased
But never caught.

We gather round the Cenotaph
Each bleak November,
The torch of freedom
Now a glowing ember.
And afterwards, around 'The Legion' bar
We drown our sorrows,
and talk of those who gave their all
For our tomorrows.

Could we but write some lines
That would withstand the ravages of time
To reign sublime,
or will our story grace some dusty shelf
unread - until we're dead.

M F Parkinson

Old Lady

Old Lady in the window seat,
Why feel you your fingers?
The left index pointed to her chosen one,
Hair slicked, light footed
Dancer.
To join her,
To Father her child.
Watching him grow,
Grasping with chubby,
Uncontrolled hands
Her middle finger.
The band still glows,
As when in May,
'Neath blossomed bough,
He wed 'til Death
Called
In Flanders
And grief's tears
Bite, to mark
The fourth.
Old lady -
Do you recall?

D G Ellam

Yesterday's Heroes

They were only young men
As they left old Englands shores
Thousand after thousands
Sent to fight a war

It all began at Serbia
So our History says
Who are we to argue
As their assassinated royalty lie in state

Say goodbye to loved ones
Kiss your girls goodbye
No don't look back lads
There's a tear in every eye

To fight for King and country
Each one given a gun
Take a steady aim lad
Be sure to get a Hun

Anxious moments for them at home
Watching for the mail
Jack, Tom, Joe are missing
Goes the cry each day

They'll send you his medals
To wear on special days
We live in our free country
For the sacrifice they made.

Rod Marshall 3rd Battalion Coldstream Guards

Life

War, Peace, to me is life itself
The poor the hungry the people with wealth
The guns the roses the tears the smiles
The funeral parlours, the wedding aisles

The war, the gun shots and the screams
Countries no water no rivers no streams
The manor houses the cold mud huts
The wounds the gashes the grazes the cuts

The young the old, the new fresh minds
The good the bad the evil the kind
Who thought one world could have this strife
For war and peace to me is life.

Louise Fry (13)

Why Must It Be

As I was laid prone in a Normandy field
My eye on a Bren gun sight
I said to myself 'Why Must It Be'?
Why do we have to fight?

When I squeezed the trigger, a young man fell
And my blood ran cold, when I heard him yell
I thought, Good God, what have I done
I've killed some poor Mothers son.

I was a soldier 'the same as he'
But what had that poor chap done to me
I consoled myself 'it was him or me
But why? Oh why' did it have to be.

I thought of my training, 'kill or be killed'
Whilst my eyes quite soon with tears were filled
It was never explained what it was all about
Whey we had to kill men, we knew nothing about.

It's every man's duty, his homeland to defend
And I'd fight for mine right on to the end
No doubt, each soldier, has the same thought in his head
But what can you defend, once you are dead.

Men are sent into battle, their countries to save
And many get buried in a lonely grave
They've fought for their country, their duty's been done
But how do they know, if a war has been won.

Wives and parents get letters to say
Your husband 'or son', has fallen today
It's almost certain, that their grief can't be healed
So why? Oh why, did I have to lay in that field.
James Lockwood

'A Poem for Peace'

All you people with limbs and health,
Look around for those the lame.
They're the one's who gave themselves,
But they were not to blame.

And think of those who ne'er returned,
Their blood stained far and wide.
Our life and freedom they have earned,
For our children in peace to guide.

If we guide them not, in this our life,
What hope have they to see.
That wars bring only death and strife,
For all the world to be.

Tell them, show them, read
Of the sick, the dead and the lame.
Of this we want them to be freed,
Let them suffer not the same.

Our fathers suffered such as we,
Our women did that too.
So all good people, hear my plea,
As this I put to you.

Look around and guide the youth,
Teach them right from wrong.
Teach them tolerance, patience and truth,
To sing a peaceful song.

When we've taught our children this,
And hate for all does cease
When all our hearts do ring in bliss,
Then we'll have learnt to live in peace.

B Griffiths

Wounded

'Bale Out', and with no delaying,
On Terra Firma, but which way out?
A pause behind the stricken tank,
With bullets zipping, striking, hurting:
Where to dodge the lethal curtain?
Survival's what it's all about.

A furtive dash into deserted homes,
Searching for a friendly face,
The street by now all laced with lead,
With death about for he who roams,
Along that street it has to be,
Safety the prize in a deadly race.

Bodies lying in unworldly poses,
Friend and foe sprawl in thorny hedges,
Some enemy are there alive,
Skulking in amongst the roses;
And two are shepherded away,
Hands aloft, skirting pitted roadside edges.

The Troop Commander's Tank's in view,
A head pokes out, and then inquires,
'Is anybody hurt', the officer cries,
I check myself in haste, anew,
'Yes', my answer loud and clear,
As blood begins to flow, and flesh pespires.

A hurried dash into a ditch,
And clothing's ripped away, in cover.
Where? and how bad is it all?
As blood still flows, so red and rich;
'You're on your way home my lad', they said,
As suddenly the stinging pain takes over.

Iolo Lewis

The Italian Garden

A formal garden behind an eighteenth century wall
Marble benches and vases
Ilex trees and oleanders
Gravel paths and small box hedges
- and a tiny, tinkling fountain

I went there twice with dark-haired Ida Gellini
Once in snow winter
Once in dusty summer
We walked and talked
And sat the days away
Eating black cherries and drinking chianti

She was nanny
To the children of the house
I, a young soldier
Of the occupying army

A lifetime later whenever I see
Cool marble and crunchy paths
Tall thin trees and hot sun
I think of Ida
What happened to her?
does she ever think of me?

John Dossett-Davies

As Years Go By

The passing years
Have borne away
Staunch men
Who n'eer forgot the day,
When fending hard a foe
Did terrors share
With those who came not home
But sleep they there!

The sun which heralds day
With every dawn
Shines down on rows
Of marking stones
Where men in peace now lie,
Lights up the names of all
Engraved there on
Touches at home
A soul who yet may sigh!

Bill Rowan S/Sgt Royal Engineers

Memories

A young, well-tanned Major arrived, looking so squeaky-clean,
It made us soldiers wonder, if he had ever been
Where it was dirty ... Till we heard that he had an M.C.
Gained fighting in North Africa - Tobruk I think. - Now he

Took us in hand. We trained as we had never trained before.
We sweat and strained our guts out and gasped and groaned and
                                                        swore.
'All things at the double, men ... Don't walk but always run,
You have to be fit warriors for when you meet the Hun.'

He had some odd ideas and disliked facial hair.
No beard! No moustache! For bad germs gathered close in there.
'You can chase the German now, with the training you've been
                                                        given.
And if God takes you shaved, might forgive you being unshriven.'

'Go with a hair-free face, if He should call your name.' -
Ad he did, leading his company. He was not to blame.
It was the Brigadier, sent us against Hun tanks
Hull-down in a Hamlet- across snow - and little thanks

To his staff. The sited tanks almost shattered the attack.
Only thirty of us reached them before they could pull back.
The ground was littered with us. The churned snow coloured red
As we checked our fallen later. Eight-nine and most were dead.

I saw our Odd-ball Major. His face half-dirty now
But peaceful, mute in death and not a furrow in his brow.
His corpse, a mess for tanks Hull-down can deal a lot of harm!
Despite the blood and carnage, he lay there still and calm.

112

It's almost half a century since that unpleasant time
And ponder why, at eighty, I'm scribbling this in rhyme?
Perhaps his 'In memoriam' is, in a kind of way,
That rain or shine, well or ill, I shave clean every day.

G Bristow

Bananas

Our kid got leave from the navy,
he'd got a surprise for our mam,
a great tree of bananas, but as he got off of the tram,

The kids came running from nowhere,
all followed him home to our street.
He looked like the flippin' pied piper,
taking the kids for a treat.
He looked down at the little faces all lifted up in awe,
They'd never seen a banana, only pictures before.

So every child was given one,
then clutching it in their hands,
said 'Thanks mister, we'll go and show our mams'
but only one banana was left for our mam.

Joan Littlehales

Dunkirk

Old river steamers
With old Whiskered Skippers
Ploughed through stormy waters
To face a vicious foe.
For Britain's youth was waiting.
Waiting, and Praying.
Crowded on the beaches
With no where else to go.

Old battered Steamers,
Their useful lives near ending.
Whistled their arrival
As they reach the Dunkirk Shore.
There, among the big ships,
The tiny boats and Steamers,
Risked all, to reach these young men
And bring them home once more.

Old rusty river Steamers.
Their useful lives now over.
Lie beached and are forgotten.
Their Valiant Skippers too.
But we - remembering Dunkirk
And that Land of Glory.
Give thanks to those small Steamers.
Their Skippers, and their Crew.

Dorothie Stalton A.T.S. R.E.M.E.

116

Journeys End

Steam hissing grinding screeching wheels,
And voices echoing shrill and high
About the grimy station roof,
And sunlight struggling through the gloom
Casting long nets of light and shade
Upon the shifting aimless throng.

There on each face emotion traced,
Mirrored the surging of the heart,
Watching the fingers on the station clock
Creep slowly nearer to that breathless hour,
For anticipation made the weary minutes drag
In a bitter foretaste of eternity.

Now from the open sliding doors
The men whom war had tossed aside
Were disgorged on the platform there,
With empty sleeves and pain wracked eyes,
Limping, grasping comrades arms
They came into the waiting crowd.

There were no bands or waving flags,
Just tears, and familiar outstretched arms,
And voices hushed in sympathy
As through the station door they passed
Jesting ironically at the poster there
'Was your journey really necessary?'

J A Brown

Convoy at Sunset

Not daring ride alone the nightmare sea,
We've raised a terror worse than the awful storm
Our forebears feared: grouped against the submarine,
We plod along and trust we see the dawn.

Like burr of wind in a tower's peak
Up unbattened hatches destroyer's engines whine,
Bringing a poky smell of seamen's sleep,
A clang of seaboots down its armoured mine.

Beneath black vats and naked bulbs and pipes,
Where needles, din-shocked, gauge correctly,
A deafened stoker, taking cotton, wipes
The sweat off, pensively but quickly.

Down in the glow of messdecks greasy fists
Are fumbling cards or scribing to a girl;
Aloft in the dusk the helmsman's swinging wheel
Keeps our forepeak doggedly a-West.

Nostalgic accordion sounds across the water,
Pipes aglow, while soft eyes gaze;
In armour's iron the heart is very tender;
Noon's firm horizons fade in evening haze.

Sunsets in rigging of cargoboats,
Flower-named trawlers, English harbour,
Mirth and ale at *The Hearts of Oak*,
Love's gentle greeting in a warm parlour,

Now is it our ocean foe reclaims
Gruff lads hammocked in fleeting iron.
We lift and lurch, crammed in uneaseful dreams
And long - O God! - to see the golden dawn.

A R Home

RDC92

The Reality of War

It is easy to talk of glory friend, and say we are in the right,
And shout 'God strafe the enemy, and lets put him to flight'.
But let us first consider, before we start to fight,
The reality of War.

Did you ever stand by the Troopers rail, and hear the klaxons blare,
And hear the boom of impending doom, and see the Tanker flare.
And hear the screams of her drowning crew as they swum in a sea of
flame.
That my friend is War.

Did you ever stand in the desert sand close by a refuelling troop,
And hear the crack of an eighty eight, and see the Stuka swoop.
And see the flash of exploding bombs as the Valentine brews up.
That my friend is War.

Did you ever stand on the minefields edge, and watch the Sappers
creep,
And see them make their one mistake, and the deadly Tellers leap.
Then see the mangled Swaddy as he lay in his lasting sleep.
That my friend is War.

Did you ever stand midst falling walls, as the Dorniers made their
pass,
With the firemen sticking to their posts among the splintering glass.
Then helped dig out infant bodies in the grisly aftermath.
That my friend is War.

So talk no more of war my friend or couple it with fame,
It never was a pleasure, and certainly no game.
So let us pray to God above that war may be no more.
And that Peace may reign.

S Dollimore Ex R.C.M.P.

121

Stars and Crowns

A Subaltern to his Lady-love

'Tis not these stars of bronze I wear,
　Dear love, upon my shoulder
That make me in the battle dare
　Things hazardous and bolder.

Nor think that visions of the crown
　Of higher rank enthral me.
Something more precious than renown
　To doughty deeds doth call me.

'Tis not these stars: it is thine eyes
　That thrill me to my duty.
The crown I dream of, and my prize,
, Is thou, thy love and beauty.

Norman Hurst

Wartime at Sea

I stood my watch with heavy heart
The ship was bathed in spray,
Last night was just a start...
The pack were here to stay.

The merchantman that had been sunk
Was in it's watery grave...
Her lone survivor, in his bunk...
The rest we could not save.

The escort crew were tired... and angry too
At all the blood and gore,
Our God it seemed, had deemed it so
But Lord... what was it for?

Upon the bridge I gazed and then...
Thought of the U Boats down below,
Why were men... killing men...
And boys who'd never grow?

Our ship had guns and means to kill
The dreaded boats beneath...
Though they like us would have their fill
But dream of home and heath.

Onwards our convoy braved the sea
Each mile was counted thus...
Dear Lord, should you take care of me
Then, why not all of us?

Peter Seaborn Ex R.N.

France to Burma, 1940 - 1944

An army in retreat is not a pretty sight,
Made up of all the elements of flight:
A Staff Officer, the pompous sort,
Who demanded all my maps,
Because the General was short!
My CO, at the RV, said 'well done,
I'm glad I'm not you, the world's gone mad,
Take off your boots and have a sleep my lad.'
The tanks, unaccountably, came from the South,
They blocked the road. The SS were uncouth.
There was a gap in the roadside hedge,
I dived thro and lay still.
The abject column trudged on, the MG at the rear passed,
I made for the woods.
A French boy barely ten approached,
Shyly he handed me his lunch of bread,
'Bon chance Monsieur', he said.
Years later on Pagoda Hill, a river at our back,
Tired of retreat we awaited the attack.
They came as dawn broke and overran our first outpost,
They seemed to infest the hillside, hidden in the tall grass.
For two hours we held on, though ordered back.
Our last burst was aimed at the Rising Sun,
'Twendé Majaliwa', I murmured to my companion, for he was black.
Ki Swahili for 'Let's go.'

James Stevenson

Desert Elegy

Above the silent desert sands,
The kite hawks soar and fly,
Where burned out tanks and cannon point;
Dead fingers' at the sky.

No longer is the sky at night,
Lit up with rocket trails so bright,
Where hardly time to draw a breath,
Brings agony and sudden death,

The contestants all have gone away,
Another war, another day,
Until the oil wells again will burn,
We do not care, we never learn.

Why all this sacrifice of life?
The reason must be told,
For beneath these vast desert wastes,
Lie oceans of black gold.

Ronald Duck

Young Johnny

Young Johnny marched against his will
He knew that death lurked o'er the hill.
The drums beat firmly as he walked,
While some few soldiers coolly smoked.

Forward they pressed, a stuka dived,
They lay there flat, but four men died.
As there he lay deep in the ditch,
Young Johnny, hypnotised, bewitched.

Again they pressed on through the smoke,
That had been cover for the hawk.
They kept on in their weary way,
And did not rest till end of day.

The morning came with sudden shock.
A burst of fire hit a rock.
A lonely sniper slid away,
As a British Soldier wounded lay.

A Spandau coughed a deadly arc,
And every bullet found its mark.
The Huns, they crouched low in their nest.
Their smoking gun had done the rest.

D W Humphreys

The Spitfire

The brave, late-Autumn sun shed a kindly glow
On the green-capped, grey-white cliffs, till they spilled down
A pale gold cascade into the rippling serene
Sea-born reflection of a bright blue sky.

High in the heavens the hate of hell droned death,
Death dropping suddenly, screaming down from the skies,
Down with blasting, blinding, shattering explosion:
Friends' fury, hate of humanity, hating Christianity.
Christ! Art thou sleeping? Lo, the little town's
Loved women and children martyred, mangled lie,
By satanic maniac blow.

Fierce, frightening, angrily flashing avenging wings
Sweep from the blue with the swiftness of the wrath of God.
The chattering, punishing-death-with-death, heart-seeking,
                                            heart-finding
Hail of lead remorselessly stabs, stabs, stabs.
The hell-hound in death-throes writhing plunges down.

Ah, brave, bright-silvered wings, soar on in the sunshine.
Take up again the Archangel Michael's task
Of scouring the heavens of the sullying legions of evil,
Making once more our English sky above us
Meet to be numbered amongst the realms of God.

Folkestone December 1940.

Leo Davis

To the Western Desert

Oh desert you owe me a debt,
You owe me youthful years,
Full three and more you made me sweat,
You drank my blood and tears.

The very fact that you exist
Was bad enough before
We foreigners ground out the grist
On your plains just made for war.

One thing I'll grant - that you were fair -
To none you gave succour,
You were impartial to despair,
Men could not hate thee more.

I used to sit and curse the sun
In those far off desert days,
I set forth as each day begun
To sweat beneath its rays.

But I escaped your barren waste,
Your fruitlessness I spurn,
I could not leave with greater haste,
I swore I'd not return.

And yet sometimes when I think back,
Once more I'd tread your rock,
And ride along the vanished track;
Your mirage I would mock.

Let not nostalgia woo my soul,
Your mirage holds your purse,
You took men's lives instead of toll -
You still deserve my curse.
Frank Paul Ex R.A.F.

128

Flag Day

They walk towards me, short-sighted,
Peering at the banner and the box.
Something behind the eyes closes.
Uncomfortable.
Men have died. Been injured.
Messy. Best forgotten
Better to spend the money
On wide-eyed animals
And images on small screens.

There is no media-hysteria
In putting money in a plastic box
For war-torn heroes packed away
In unseen wards
Of unknown hospitals.

The old though. The pensioners.
Men in threadbare coats
With only pennies in a plastic bag.
Wheelchair veterans
Of other wars
And widows of those wars.

They remember them.

Elsie M Torrent

The Blitz

I well recall the days of the Blitz,
Those terrible days, we were 'hammered' by 'Fritz',
The skies over London were *black, with* the *shadows*
Of bombers, who sought to put London to *ash.*

The people were valiant, the one that were spared
Their bravery legend, the deeds that were shared,
The enemy tried, but we would not be bowed,
By a nation of tyrants, our spirits not cowed.

The horror of bombings, the terror of fire,
The warnings, the 'blackout' the sound of gunfire,
The black pall of smoke and the terrible smell,
The water from hoses the flames for to quell.

But for all of its batterings, our city survived,
It picked up the pieces - got on with its life,
We finally won, at a terrible cost,
But what would we be if the battle we'd lost.

Joan Wheeler

Near Tournai - May 1940

The curve of the ball thrown in from extra-cover,
When they've taken their one and know they can take no more,
The lazy climb to the top and the sharp turn-over
Down to the wicket; - that is how I saw
The flight of the hand-grenade from the rifle-cup
Over the Escaut canal to the shrubby ground
In front of the railway line; and its sharp black sound
Was the burst of applause which her lads the fifty up.
When I had time to think it was often thus -
One of the new strange sights would take me away
To the old and well-loved things which happened to us
In the quiet years before the rest of the fray,
Before peace-loving men turned rancorous,
In the quiet years which will come again some day.

John Biddell Ex Border Regiment

Our First Air-Raid

The wailing siren sounds its urgent cry
For everyone to leave their work or play,
And hurry to the shelter, as a high
Explosion rents the air not far away.
So everywhere the sound of rushing feet
And each stunned face displays an anxious hue.
The war has come to our once peaceful street
Now we must find the strength to see it through.

John Parfett

Sparrows Nest

There's a stone and bronze memorial
stands facing out to sea
To the men whose lives were sacrificed
in 'Harry Tate's Navy'.

A bronze ship reflects their glory
high above the Sparrows Nest
More inscriptions bear the names of all
whose souls were called to rest.

They came from every quarter
they seasoned sailor, the naive,
Drawn together to a destiny
where death held no reprieve.

A Royal Navy within a Navy
bloody-minded to the last
Born of guts and determination
strong, belligerent, steadfast.

In converted fishing trawlers
Whalers, drifters, men so brave
Would never more return to shore
as the sea became their grave.

There's a silver badge of courage
worn with pride and dignity
By the men who scoured the oceans
wide and kept the sea-lanes free.

In Remembrance of their shipmates
from experience they at best
Can reciprocate with honour
the Glorious Might of Sparrows Nest.
June Pledger

Normandy

It was a dark and stormy night
When we launched our main attack
With our belly's filled with fright
We stormed the falaise gap.

As the guns began to fire
And shells started to scream
We struggled on through the mire,
As in a horror dream.

We saw our comrades hit and fall
Sightless eyes looked to the sky
To save mankind they gave their all
Twenty was too young to die

At St Desir now lies my brother
With his cousin by his side
In battle they came together
And side by side they died.

Now the battles have been won
And France once more is free
Are they just a mother's son
Who died for you and me.

B T Phillips

March 13th 1940

I came to Melton Mowbray long ago,
When war-time's strict blackout darkened the town.
Spears of driving, icy rain slanted down,
And cold, piercing winds wildly threatened snow.

Down Burton Road my weary feet dragged, slow
And aching legs took me past Church and Crown,
Through the dark widespread skirts of night's black gown,
And I paused to wonder: Where could I go?

Wearily I walked up Nottingham Road,
And found a hidden spot where I could rest;
And freezing rain turned into threatened snow!

Holwell works all night digested its load,
While I fitfully slept. But I possessed
A sixteen year old's resilience and go!

Dan Pugh

Officer Cadet

To be a soldier and attempt the poet
Seems an incongruity. I know it
Has been done; but the nauseating smell
Of powder - the heave - the lift - 'tis hell
To prate verbose in this pollution.
More fame to stun the Colonel with the 'school solution.'

Gordon Carter

Sussex

All this is mine - the downs, the cliffs that stand
As they have stood since Time was not,
The strong sweet scent of thyme, the sheep bells far
Upon the distant hills, the little plot
That is God's Acre and the little
Crooked path that runs to Jevington.
And if I do not see this land again - what matters it?
One need not see to love, and I will gladly go
If by my going I can feel assured
That in the future still the winds will blow
To peaceful folk, the sounds of hone on scythe
And bells in West Dean Church that praise the Lord.

Mary Hughes

Arakan 1945

The jewelled sky towards the east
Still flashes like an amethyst
With golden veins; nor has ceased
To hope the butterfly its lover's tryst
With heavy waxen blooms to keep.
Swift grows the dark. Upon the hill
The old pagoda seems to sleep,
Wrapped in mystery - silent, still.

Beneath, the jungle comes to life
And men, like beasts, in fox-holes lie
While fear, that sharp-edged knife,
Cuts deep. Tonight, perhaps, they die.
But thoughts, annihilating space,
Their oft-trod journey make
To raise again the vision of a face
Well-loved and ease again their hearts of ache.

J R Allan

When it's Over

Will I recall Parades at cold grey dawn;
Right dressing, numbering and forming threes,
Top-coated, noses red and faces drawn;
The joke, that 'Stand at ease' meant 'Stand and freeze'?

Will I recall the noisy Dining Hall
The clatter of the plates; the ready wit?
Will I forget the laughter, of us all,
The first day we were issued with our kit?

Will I recall that first return from leave;
Those few mute moments just before 'Goodbye';
The hurried wipe of eyes upon the sleeve;
The twisted smile; the awful urge to cry?

Will I recall those endless 'Naafi' queues
For two sale buns, a cup of tepid tea;
Or shall I, when it's over, rather muse
On comradeship that meant so much to me?

The ever helping hand - the friendly grin
The latest joke we passed from lip to lip:-
Out of the muck of war we all were in
I found a precious jewel - Comradeship

W G Harrison

141

The Transport Girls of the ATS

Twenty of us to a hut
sitting on soldiers boxes..in our undies
making up for evening dates or dances
chattering like magpies
seventeen to thirty plus, blondes, brunettes, redheads
country girls, town girls, shy girls, confident girls
the ATS drivers...
and we drove everything.. alongside the lads
staff cars, PU's, TCV's, water carriers, six ton fords,
Fifteen hundred weights three ton Bedfords, motor bikes..
on convoy..bringing back unit returns..on which nothing worked,
in Winter.. freezing in the old water carriers
we called 'coffins'
canvas sides, window paned sized windscreens..
clad in leather jerkins, boots, gaiters, gauntlets
our 'badge'.. the strap of our caps
proudly worn..over the top
we loved our job
took pride in a shining vehicle
carried out inspections and repairs, changed oil,
drained stop cocks at night, in Winter
emerged from underneath trucks grimy with grease... yet
spick and span..in tunic and skirt
at the salute
when driving the Brigadier or Colonel
proud of our job
proud of our reputation
still proud of our record
the drivers of the ATS

Pat Bates (Formerly Col. Pat Morgan)

Britains Pride

Now listen! All parents and families too,
We'll tell you the story of out love for you,
For we are the reason why you live free now,
We taught, fed, and loved you, we showed you the way
And gave you the knowledge between right and wrong,
We helped you through life as you travelled along.

We were Britains Navy who fought on the sea
And guarded our sailors in the Merchant Navy,
We were Britains Armies, at home and abroad
Who fought and defeated the enemy horde,
We were Britains Air Force, the many, the *few*
Who defeated and shattered, those opposing, who flew.

We women did our share as Wrens, and as ATS
We served with our Airmen int he ranks of the WAAFS
We mothers did wonders with rations so small
Took the place of our men folk who heard Britains call
With nights in bomb shelters and days at our work
We sang as we laboured, no danger did shirk.

The cost of our victory our loved ones gave
Their lives by the million our lives to save.
God rest them and keep them in eternal peace
Our memories of them never shall cease
The debt that we owe them we still owe today
While our lives in freedom continue to stay.

Now may years on, as we fade away,
Our hearts still unbowed, though our heads may be grey
You owe it to us, that you live free today
Remember, remember, that when we are gone
We leave it to you, to still carry on
The fight for the right for our England.
Walter H N Charman

World War Two

The horrors and the grief of war
can never be forgot,
The men who suffered, wives despaired
The children they begot
All these are scarred, though years ago
These men and women faced the foe.

The Dunkirk epic, when we stood
Alone against the Hun,
The miracle of little boats
A dangerous job well done.
The skies above our island too
Defended by the gallant 'few'!

'D' day after gruesome years
Renewed our hope, we prayed
That soon the death, the horror, fear
Might truly be allayed.
Our allies suffering, death camps where
The Jews had tyranny to bear.

At last the daring Arnhem 'op',
would this now end the war?
The gallantry of those brave few
Against the Panzers' roar!
'Twas not to be, they were betrayed
They fought and died, a great price paid!

Eventually the light prevailed
The Allies did win through,
But Second World War memories
Still with us, do renew
old memories, with the Legion's aid
Our debt to these men should be paid.
Betty Simpson

Air-Raid

Dawn glows like an almandine
Set in the rich town's mayoral chain.
Oh, what in the red arising are those birds nine
Foretelling me and mine amongst the slain?

In far-off elfin mirth the stars and sea
(Whom none hear in our buzz of day)
Ate telling, too, that Death is free,
Would make his liberators pay.

But spirit warnings miss the ken
Of ones deat-mute from merchant sounds:
Airs too light for milling men,
Serious, proud, eyes glued to the ground.

And so the bombers darkened the sky like bors,
And drails of bombs went angling the earth for souls,
With flashes, thunder, flinders, screaming horrors.
Death-ruckle of masonry falling in holes.

The corpses in our city clan
Could never, living, comprehend
How heart's trust sold to fellow man
Precipitates this Godless end.

J L Harmsworth

Two Minutes Silence

It is when, the strong are weak
The weak are strong
The mighty are humble
The humble are mighty
The mightiest pay tribute
And rulers obey
The captive are free
And the free are captive
It is when, the armless salute
The legless stand
The sightless see
And mothers weep
While we stand among poppies

Jack Guthrie

When You Come Walking in

Loving hands will welcome you
When you come walking in
Loving eyes will sparkle
With the old familiar gleam,
Loving hearts with joy will beat
The dear returning one to greet,
Hear the sound of hastening feet,
When you come walking in.

We have missed you all the while
From our little Home-land Isle,
We have watched your vacant chair
Wishing, wishing you were there,
Missed your foot upon the stair
Missed your whistles of latest air,
But out of the window flies dull despair
When you come walking in.

The birds do sing, the sun does shine,
The home becomes a treasured shrine,
Everything in lovely rhyme
When you come walking in
E'en though we have to part again
We shall take a fresh heart again,
Happy memories to retain;
Love will be our glad refrain
Hope will live till once again
You come walking in.

Elizabeth Towne

From the Regular to the Civvy Attached

I'm just an old soldier, with time still to do,
For Demob: and Repat:, I've no need to queue,
When others have gone, I'll still be here,
Drinking my monthly ration of beer,
But when I get home, I'll most likely meet,
Some of those others in Civvies so neat,
Maybe I'll smile, I hope they will too,
When they see an Old soldier, with time still to do.

Although an old soldier, with time still to do,
I'm still young and healthy, as good as new,
Don't think I'm Grousing or shooting aline,
I think the Civvies have done their job fine,
But give them their jobs, I'll stick to mine,
Be it in India or back on the Rhine,
Some have signed on to a life that's quite new,
Now, like me they have still time to do.

It is the old soldier with time still to do,
Who keeps some from starting a riot or two,
In places you others have fought for and won,
Before we put Jerries and Japs on the run,
Together we beat them right down to their knees,
So, lets stick together, I'm asking you please,
When you get home, and start life anew,
Remember the ones, who have still time to do.

B Simmons 11th E.A. Division

South Atlantic Convoy - 1940

Trapped, encircled by endless seas,
I watched those jostling waves of fire
embrace a symphony of colour,
where, leaping with the elemental dare
of flying fish,
flashes of silver
arched through deepening dusk.

While ahead, apart,
coded signals winked to port.

Frank Pittman

London's Burden 1940

London that did shine by night
With flickering lights, and neon signs
But all this now has gone from sight
As though some land has drawn the blinds

The greatest city on the sphere
Has now and always been so dear
But now it has a job to do
'Gainst screaming death from or the blue.

For every night when day has ended
A droning sound comes from up high
and mingled with it also blended
a warbling note gives reason why!

From over our encircling sea
The murderous Hun in bombers fly
Just to frighten you and me
But our big guns give him reply.

Try as he may to make us break
We still smile up and give brave face
For he has made a bad mistake
How can he smash so great a race.

Over he comes to bomb the people
And meeting him is thundering gun
Houses, buildings, flats, tall steeple
He then turns, his work is done.

But does he know what he had hit
For people live within those homes
But they don't cry their full of gait
Even if they're broken bones.

But there will come a time when we
Shall get revenge upon this Fritz.
For all we think of victory
And parring off, this Hun's Blitz.

and soon when brighter days are here
When sun will shine after the rain
And ending all with song and clear
London's lights will shine again.

H W (Bill) Ford

Victory in Defeat

Despite all attempts to relieve them
We had to call it a day
The Germans were massing their forces
Growing stronger every day
Our vital line of communication
Was under permanent threat
We couldn't get up enough supplies
and so he scene was set

The Paras were to be withdrawn
Under cover of the night
They were ferried across the river
It was a tragic sight
For they had fought and given their all
Men refusing to be cowed
They'd brought honour to Regiment and country
all of them could be proud

It had been a desperate gamble
Which very nearly came to fruition
We had nothing to be ashamed of
We'd done well as a Division
But as Napoleon learned - much to his cost
when forced to retreat from Moscow
Without a good line of communication
The cold wind of defeat will blow

I remember I wrote a letter back home
Shortly after the event
It was full of praise for the Paras
For they'd been magnificent
They earned the name 'Red Devils'
Were praised throughout the land
'If you spot a red beret' I wrote to my Mom
'Go and shake him by the hand'

J Newman

Weary of War

World War I, a war to end all wars is what they said,
Never again to fight and leave so many young men dead.
World War II and there was conflict yet again,
How could we suffer once more those years of pain.

On land and on the sea and also in the air,
Men fought and died, it mattered not where.
Women and their children and the aged also died,
Bombs killing thousands leaving millions to cry.

Six whole years of deprivation and terror,
We found prison camps, and saw with such horror
Mans abusement of his fellows had known no bounds,
Yet all we could do was utter sympathetic sounds.

After all this time have we learned any more?
Men are still sent to fight someone else's war.
Mothers, wives and children still shed their tears,
Offer prayers and plead for peace, but who hears?

Perhaps one day common sense will prevail,
and we will know that fighting is all to no avail.
Then man will live in peace with man for evermore,
When we have learned to know the pure futility of war.

Joyce Shinn

A Soldiers War

Bloody fields disguised with aloe spire,
Bodies, torn and bleeding, on barbed wire.
The cannon belch their cordite smell,
The stench of death, that once were men.
Oh, what a glorious battle boys.

The general sits a rear his troops,
Not quite the story you read in books.
For only the standard is flying high,
As all around him his young men die.
Oh, what a glorious battle boys.

The once green fields run red with blood,
Of a mothers, sisters, sweethearts love.
For our pain and suffering is mortal made,
In politicians office, where plans are laid.
Oh, what a glorious battle boys.

It's us, not they, with best friends maimed,
Orphaned children, their young lives changed.
False vanities hurt more than pride,
You don't enlist to commit suicide.
Oh, what a glorious battle boys.

A broken form comes limping home,
With bandaged head and clothes all torn.
'It's o'er,' he cries. 'I've made men die,
But no-one will answer my question, why?'
Oh, what a glorious battle boys.

Colin Knowles

Horse Transport

Horses are not for war.
Perhaps for the sabre-slash
of the hunting-field,
or a white-lathered dash
into claythick farmyards,
or the soft-silver slide
of Imperial Reviews.

But not for the uphill slog
as pack-transport,
the noise, mud, shell-sliver
scream of beast panic
as artillery-fire rains down.

Their soft quivering noses
are too pure, too soft,
too velvety-kind.
Only Man deserves
brute suffering.

Colin McIntyre

The Invasion

England, land of my hopes, fears, sorrows and joys
England, land of the free.
Whose very soul is stirred
When winds, waves and foe are dared
By men of all lands
Whose common purpose is to see this through.

Thoughts may bring doubts
Of England's kindness to her kin
In Peace. But war unites -
No man may stand aside from this
With that full knowledge, which springs from love,
We take our place beside our forbears,
Whose proud traditions live and challenge our weakness.

Draw strength then from our Island's tale.
Fail not where they succeeded.
To die is but to die - no more.
It is the spirit which one dies with.

Pray hard for strength and it shall come
And at long length, the battle won
Tired and worn,
Yet shall there be reborn
An England which doth show the way
To high achievement for the promised day.

Lines sent to his wife by the late Sgt William Newby Thomson
(R.A.M.C.)

W N Thomson

Normandy

Here I sit - all on my own.
With no one to talk to
Only the drone of the warlike craft
To keep my mind upon these dreary days of war.

Was it yesterday, or the day before
We talked and made our plans
Of what we'd do of where we'd go,
When these mad days were gone.

Just twenty odd years, give or take a few days,
Our ages where the same
Full of hope - and love, and fear,
All lads alike, except in name.

Was is yesterday or the day before,
we shared each others sorrow,
Found courage to face the unknown task,
The filth - the stench - the horror.

On sentry go at dead of night,
We would often be together;
I expect 'twill be the same tonight,
Tho' many have gone forever.

We were with them at the end,
Their untimely shattering deaths,
We did our best to comfort them,
Will remember them - till our last breath.

These men we were proud to have as friends,
Their deeds of valour cherish;
Why do so many stay alive?
Why do so many perish?

This war has taught me many things,
The rewards that come from strife,
What a true comrade really is,
How precious is a life.

R Clarke (Ex 4th Bn Kings Shropshire Light Infantry)

On Hearing the News
'There was some damage to property'

Weep not for those whose silver pointed wings
Rode winds and storms to conquer the deep sky,
Who conversed with the stars, bade lightnings
And thunders on their distant errands fly;
For those who went swift or patient feet
To set their swords across the path of fate,
or kept stern vigil in some storm wracked fleet;
For youth triumphant in the gates of death.

But these poor weary ones, whose pitiful store
Of all their lives long garnering is gone,
Whose frail and careworn hands must toil once more,
Not fold in rest, the tired eyes face the sun;
These homeless, helpless ones, the cast aside,
Who will not weep for these for whom youth died.

Peter Thomas

Remembrance

Who were these men
Whose names are carved in stone?
They did not give their lives in war
But had them snatched away, before
The dreams they often talked about
In tent, on messdeck, in dug-out
Could be made real, could be fulfilled
The dreamer's dreams for ever stilled.

What were those dreams?
All had a common thread.
They dreamed of home, and child, and wife;
Living a long and happy life:
A fairer share of life's good things;
The happiness that comfort brings;
A calm old age, among their folk
Free from fear of poverty's yoke.

So, should we march?
They hated all parades.
Especially on their day of rest
When, all alike in service best,
They marched to church, where padres prayed
That peace would not be long delayed.
A prayer that struck a fervent chord
In those conscripted to the sword.

What better way
To honour all our dead?
Search out their kin, and when they're found
Comfort and aid them, all year round.
Relieve their years, sad and alone
Whose surnames too are carved in stone.

C Elkins

Post Mortem

The bugle echoes die away,
Parades dismiss and poppies fade;
Another day, another year,
Another age speeds on its way.
Forgive me, Lord, if mists of time, like battle smoke,
Bedim the features of those brave souls
Who fell beside us in those far-off fields.
We feel their presence still -
At sunrise and in the quiet hour.
'For God, King and country!' Ay, we remember well -
We snatched the banner from their dying hands
And bore it thro' to final victory.
Forgive us Lord, if that sacred trust they left us
Seems slipping from our grasp, whilst we watch helplessly
As their proud legacy wastes with us day by day.
What did we buy with lives so young and fair?
Forgive me Lord, for I am frail and spent,
But never let me dare to think
They may have died in vain.

Roy Smith

164

Escape to Wisden

News from the Gulf ... more pain and wretchedness;
More horrors flashing hourly on the screen;
More lives destroyed - I switch off in distress,
Scanning my Wisden shelves, calm fields of green.

Switched off ... I fondle '1891',
Escaping back one hundred years ago,
Feasting on Grace, Briggs, Shrewsbury and Gunn;
Safe from our modern catalogue of woe.

'The Golden Age' - I turn the years, engrossed
With 'Ranji', Fry, Rhodes, Trumper, Bosanquet -
Joining that far off 'soundless-clapping host'
Convinced their world's bright sun would never set.

Through thickening volumes, boasting peace and plenty,
Age of the Raj, securely I proceed;
Through years romanticized by G. A. Henty,
On to the youthful Hobbs, Hearne, Woolley, Mead.

Then four thin, shrivelled Wisdens break the spell:
No hard-fought Tests now, waged with bat and ball.
The green fields yield to bloodied fields of Hell.
Four volumes paint the grimmest 'Test' of all.

The Great, the lesser and the scarcely known
Stand in The Roll of Honour, for the scythe
By which a generation's youth was mown
Embraced Brooke, Beasley, Hutchings, Neale, Booth, Blythe.

Escaping back from Wisden, I reflect
Upon the message of those death-filled shelves:
Each Golden Age is fated to be wrecked.
The fault? The fault is surely in Ourselves.
Morgan Dockrell (With kind permission of 'The Cricketer'.)

165

DVC92

Privilege

Memories of the years of war,
Of horrors and destruction,
The endless, useless waste of lives,
the courage and the suffering.

Yet thought recalls the finest hours,
Heroic deeds and valour
In travail and despair,
Light-hearted wit and humour.

Such times bring forth
Man's ultimate endeavour,
Keeping alive the gratitude
For the privilege of sharing,
The dangers and experience
Of the best of human caring.

C H Hayward

Homecoming

The soldier advances down the avenue
Sparks flashing from shined army footwear,
Gaunt, wasted, his pack almost too great a burden
He steps tall, his cap set at the correct angle

The girls watch; they've given up
Leaping with excitement at the approach
Of every khaki-clad frame, but they stop their game
Of bays, pause once more

He passes them, indifferent, then
Clicks open the gate at Number Nine:
This time it really is
'Daddy, daddy'

Helen Heslop

Italy 1944

April now, the growing hush of spring,
a tranquil sky above, and once again
my mind goes groping back, remembering,
to those brave, bitter, unremembered men
who watched the patient grass grow slowly green
on Tuscan hills, and felt the stir of birth
creep from the south, silent and scarcely seen,
across the tortured, mutilated earth
and kiss their foreheads with its warmer breath
while they lay waiting helplessly on death.

They haunt my April, those forgotten dead -
familiar faces, half-bewildered, pale,
with Grim-set mouths and troubled, anxious eyes,
thronging eternally behind her veil;
they haunt my April till the wakening leaf
aches like a wound and the round glistening bud
teems with a heart-break of unspoken grief,
and the clear sunlight rings a dying cry
around the empty nothingness of sky.

No April stirs them now,. The quiet strife,
year after year, of green recurring waves
ebbs and returns along the shores of life
over their richy futile, grassy graves.

This is their guerdon, to have sold their youth;
loved, hated, suffered and inflicted pain;
to deal in death, for some dim semi-truth;
and then, forgotten, to have died in vain,
to lie and listen, the eternal dead,
to other armies tramping overhead.

Rory MacKenzie

1940 - Recruitment and Beyond

With others as young I crossed a bridge.
To where would it lead?
To glory, boredom, sickness, death -
A sacrifice to greed?
For life now entered a newly found phase -
Wayward chance.
A shuttlecock caught by the gusting winds
To which to dance.

The uncertainty now of life and its living
Came to all.
Its intensity tempering one inner man -
'Press on - or fall!'
My character hardened quite firmly now,
Not gently.
Stretched by experience during a War
Immensely.

Stan Ward

They Called Them the Few

Not Passchendaile or Vimy Ridge, not Ypres or Verdun
No barbed wire or trenches, no hidden sniper's gun
Two decades of fragile peace, once more the naked fears
A promise not of better times but of blood and toil and tears
High above the white cliffs, above the down and weald
Not no man's land or Flanders, this then, the battlefield
Hamlet, lea and meadow not yet scarred by war
In that summer time awaiting the threat from alien shore
Hurricane and Spitfire stand, Merlin engines still
Not yet the call to action, but come it surely will
Soon the sky was filled with fire, soon the game was on
The tiny band would hold the line till the enemy was gone
They soared and dived to face the foe, to vanquish or to die
Young eagles dared and won the day in that blue September sky
Man and plane in combat no time to count the cost
And when the guns were silent, nigh on a thousand lost
They came from shire and city, some from distant strand
With one intent, one purpose, to defend this native land
From Biggin Hill and Tangmere and many an English field
A sudden glow of triumph when at last the hordes did yield
Immortal words were spoken to express the nation's due
Never in human conflict was so much owed to so few.

Ted Corns

The Desert Rats 1941 - 1942

The desert war was hard and long
And Lilli Marlene was the battle song
The days were grim 'neath the burning sun
With sand and flies and a red hot gun.
We pushed the Italians into the sea
And just when we thought the end would be
Rommel and his Afrika Corps
Hurled us back to the start once more.

We dug our trenches in desert sand
And that's when fate came to take a hand
The Germans gave us another name
Which will always live in the hall of fame
We slept in holes on our round tin hats
And the 'Jerries' called us the 'Desert Rats'.

'Monty' came and Alamein
And we were on the march again
Tobruk, Benghazi, and Tripoli too
Nothing but victory now would do
The rats were gnawing at Rommel's heels
And the 'Desert Fox' knew how it feels
To be chased and harried without respite
By a mighty foe who was full of fight.

Now we are old and turning grey
These ancient conflicts seem far away
Our enemies became our friends
And we hope that's where the story ends
But those who fought in the cruel sun
With knife and bayonet and red hot gun
Remember the land of sand and rocks
Where the 'Desert Rats' beat the 'Desert Fox'.

Brian Gregan

To Churchill 1943

When skies were dark and clouds were low
And tempests filled the air,
Your presence was the only glow that kept us from despair.
To you we looked for guidance o'er the path of bloody years
And yet, your only promise, was, - 'toil and sweat and tears'
But, girded with the armour of your confidence and power,
We held forth for Freedom, through the Nation's darkest hour.

Over many miles you travelled by land and sea and air,
The 'Ambassador of Justice' and free men everywhere, -
As you led us, in your wisdom, across the 'rocky waves',
Till now from out the shadows gleams the light of brighter days.
Still to you we look for guidance through the strife that lies ahead,
Ere the gangsters' dreams of conquest lie buried with their dead;
And the clarion call of 'Victory' is sounding loud and clear
For we know that you shall lead us to the Nation's greatest year.

Jock Park

DVC 92

174

Yokohama War Cemetery

As I gaze along the path
Rows and bushes apart
There's my Middi's grave at rest
Shining brass of his crest
Brave soldier there he fell
For King and Country to tell.

Sadly passing through the graves
Another private's name
Sleeping peacefully at rest
From Mum and Dad 'God Bless'
Will be missed your loving Wife
Your Daughter born last night.

Army, Navy, Air Force men
Flying by singing Wrens
Coloured Admirals in flight
Blowing winds through the night
Eternal spirits at peace
For ever till we meet.

Pamela Harrison

War and Peace

The Cornish wind blows free
buy the wild Marazion marsh,
gulls turn inward
from a tousled summer sea.

This is where the kestrel hovers
and sea holly blooms -
here stands a Cheshire Home,
founded by a Bomber-pilot with vision,
Lord G. L. Cheshire V.C.

Margaret Browne

To the Men of Dunkirk

At the time when the men came home from Dunkirk
A girl in my seventeenth year
As a nurse I was sent to assist their return
For the hospital I worked in was near

Going out in the dark in an old charabanc
With our blankets and stretcher, a dedicated few
Unprepared and unworldly to hear army slang
From the blunt and disabled yet cheerful crew

The coach came to a halt and the doors were flung back
When our eyes met a terrible scene:
Some men had no clothes and were covered with oil,
Some were lame or unable to see

Those that could speak were cursing like mad
'We had shovels and broomsticks' they said
'The Jerries were shooting with Stens' said one lad
'so we ran and we hid in a shed'

'My feet are so sore' said one sorry chap
 - Sadly later they were taken away -
He sang in the coach as we all motored back
Not knowing what the doctors would say

One boy - nose all black - had no ears left
They were burnt, like his arms, from the oil
He was handled with care - I was bereft -
As we arrived at the hospital door

They soon settled down to their hospital stay
And in spite of their terrible plight
They all rallied round and started to play
And gave me the name 'Nurse Brighteyes'

When you savour the worst that is meted to you
Then it may be part of life's plan
This message I send to all you brave few -
Time at pasture will surely be grand!

Enid Ashton

Ode to the Poppy

Not for you, the gardener's tender, loving care,
Watered and nurtured, to be shown off with pride,
Not for you to garland the fair maiden's hair,
Or carried in bouquets by the blushing bride.

War's declared upon you, amongst the wheat and oats,
Cut down by the blade, and trampled in the mud,
Like the soldiers of old in their scarlet coats,
Falling and staining the earth with their blood.

Your petals are as red as the blood that was shed,
In wars for freedom against slavery and fears,
Your eyes are as black as the young widow's weeds.
And the morning dew on your face are her tears.

One day in November, the Nation remembers,
You're the chosen one, the flower that we copy,
Worn with pride, flower of red, we remember the dead,
That one day is yours, the day of the Poppy.

Poppies on the Cenotaph, and on the lonely grave,
Worn by the silent crowd, as the country mourns,
Poppies of the Legion, above medals of the brave,
Poppies in churches, below the crown of thorns.

M P Blackwell

Great War Veteran Remembered

Old Jessie is dead now
and part of the past,
His yesterdays newspaper blows in the breeze'
the ice-cold night has snatched him at last,
Standing his tortured mind ar ease.

The corner of the clock tower is bleak,
It seems lonely as the ditches in the country,
For Old Jessie no longer lives on the street,
Nor strides up and down like a sentry.

No need of his sack rags any more,
Or even his Financial Times;
His soul is lost to the river's roar,
As the bell on the Clock Tower chimes.

Jessie has joined the ranks
of fallen men,
Cruel somme not the least
to remember,
But we shall honour them
again and again,
Every year on the 11th of November.

Rose Savage

Pond Farm Cemetery, Belgium

The youth of Ulster lie in peace,
The birds sing overhead,
Pond Farm, across the open fields
Brings tears for all to shed.

Now on a thriving harvest land,
The farmer goes his way,
Though over seventy years have passed
Yet the Ulsters - still they stay.

Tramp across the flowing corn
You will find them, side by side,
Near to the pond, beyond the trees
With Southerners they died.

Far from the Somme's fields they ventured,
God spared them til' that day,
When Belgium's call was uppermost,
They fell on muddy clay.

Hundreds of miles from Ulster's shore
From a life of quiet toil
To a hell, near Kemmel and Wytschaete
For to die on Belgian soil.

Fear not brave lads, we won't forget
The sacrifice you made
We will search and find those foreign fields
On which your red blood laid.

You lie beside your comrades
They promised you no harm,
'Twas German bullets cut you down
Where you lie, next to Pond Farm.
Ronnie Harkness

181

Sleep Softly

Sleep softly men of another age,
Of guns of war, of death, that twisted and tore
Your broken bodies, that speak no more,
Your voices stilled, your thoughts unspoken,
The cream of the country, that left heartbroken,
Those who knew and were full of sorrow
For a world that was robbed of a new tomorrow.

Sleep softly men of another age,
Our country fixed in time and stage,
As great a nation as in other days,
In different roles in different ways,
Still producing that 'precious dust',
That God given something that is just
The essence of this earth of ours,
Growing for this world its finest flowers.

Gone are your spirits to a higher destiny,
Your lifes blood spent so carelessly,
But a few seeds linger, dormant, waiting,
Now they will thrive to produce a nation,
To match your own, you Gods who walked,
So fleetingly across our land and talked
And loved and laughed and lived,
For you are only sleeping,
Dreaming of a world of peace,
Sane and happy, rich harvest reaping.
We will remember the price you paid
Sleep softly, wherever your dust is laid.

Ellen Tindall

182

Recall

The battle o'er
Long Long Ago,
When eager youth
To man-hood rushed.
Sapling graft to seasoned wood,
Part man, part boy, part real, part dream,
Baptised in War's unholy stream,
Long Long Ago.

The battle o'er
Long Long Ago,
Where olive groves
And grapevine grew,
Fireflies shone at eventide,
Burning charcoal tinged the morning air,
Bewildered peasants stopped to stare,
Long Long Ago.

The battle o'er
Long Long Ago,
Now medals tarnish
And wounds long healed;
Taut white across the scar.
And yesterday lies buried with the dead,
And green grass grows where blood ran red,
Long Long Ago.

M R M Pattison

Malta's Heroes

The harbour, like a battleground, is strewn
About with burnt-out hulks and sunken wrecks,
Distorted superstructures, buckled decks -
Grim, sculptured shapes by high explosive hewn.
Then air-raid sirens wail their doleful tune
And, in the sky, appear the blackened flecks
Of bursting shells among the growing specks
Of Stukas. Soon the sultry afternoon
Is darkened by the smoke of burning oil
And three-ton trucks come sailing through the air,
Blown like chaff by a thousand-pounder's blast.
Yet, in the harbour, volunteers still toil
To salve a precious cargo sunken there;
Such valour must surely be unsurpassed!

Bill Clayton

The Last Waltz

A ghost from long ago,
Bob Flint.

After Dunkirk,
He waltzed naked round the bedroom
With a war widow
Given six months to live.

A loud-mouth with a cheery grin
And Maurice Chevalier smile
Was Bob Flint;
Trembling in the slit-trench,
Nerves all shot to pieces
Out in Sicily.

Blonde and blue-eyed,
He knew the love of women,
But didn't want to live
When shrapnel sliced his legs off
By the bridge.

It was the last waltz,
Though he never knew it,
After Dunkirk
For Bob Flint.

No surviving widow.

Robin Ivy

The Jeep

Ugly little chariot, character of Puck,
Always into chaos, never getting stuck,
Outclimbing billygoats on mountain butts,
Cocksure and smug with General Smuts,
Policing brothel zones, parked outside bars,
Roaring, darting, bounding, for your master, Mars.
Wonder of the age, genius of the time,
Inquisitive, just the job, to war minds sublime,
Squat little killer, a tyke in noise,
All you lack is class, college-breeding, poise.
With those we might upraise you from your kicked-up dust
To be our cart of gold, instead of just
The jeep

H Horne

187

Untitled

I talked as we'd been taught,
Of how to kill the foe,
To fell with savage blow,
As we'd been told we ought.

It's ages since my speech,
I spoke as I did feel -
With youthful, headstrong zeal,
And thinking I could preach.

While I so warned the Hun,
My grandma, sad to hear
Such words, did volunteer:
'He too's some mother's son.'

Harry Elvidge

Normandy Harbour

Last light and permission to withdraw at last received,
The infantry dug in, their trenches like open graves we say
Must keep their short night watch alone and unrelieved
For we are too blind and vunerable to stay.

The grey tanks move slowly off the track
And spread along high Norman hedgerow.
Each crew tired now but happy to be back,
To settle for one night and not think of tomorrow.

Troop by troop they harbour by the trees
Shadows in the fading light,
The engine dies leaving for a moment still the clamour on the ears,
The radio's incessant noise 'til that too ceases, to give delicious quiet.

Crews dismount, stretching cramped limbs, feeling the earth again,
Eyes red rimmed from dust and straining in the sun,
Ever watching, ever searching with the ever present strain
Watching for the tiger, the SP and the gun.

Now, like troopers in the past we tend our steed
Waiting for the Echelon who somehow find us without fail.
No trumpet now to call up 'water and feed',
Its petrol, ammo, ration packs and mail.

Maintenance and eating done
Blankets down at last with silent thanks O Lord,
For I shall see tomorrows sun
And sleep tonight above and not like some we knew, beneath the
                                                            sward.

Rex Jackson

A Farewell to Friends

The time is drawing near
When I must leave good friends.
Soldiers I spent long years with,
On a road with many bends

And as I sail for homeward
On the sea of an ebbing tide
I'll turn and watch them standing there,
On the land I left behind

In the years of my recollections,
Those faces will grow so dim.
They will fade like the Suns reflection,
As the light of my days close in

Old pals may sometimes wonder,
Where I should one day be.
Chance meeting perhaps to ponder
When I left them by the sea.

W P Protheroe

Unknown Warrior

The desert sun dies red upon the rim
The cross's shadow falls along the grave
A rusted helmet is the symbol grim
That marks the restplace of the brave.

No other landmark mars the sandy scene
The ground runs dismal to the sky
No sign of life, no bright oasis green
The wind's hushed voice is but a hopeless sigh.

How died this soldier far from brother men
Who laid him last to rest beneath the soil
Who wished to keep him within earthly ken
When war had put to end his mortal toil.

Andrew Todd

Requiem for Dead Trees

Dedicated to the aftermath of a night during which our position was
subject to incessant Japanese mortar-fire, and serves as a corollary to
the bombing of cities, in which the innocent become the victims.
Nagkedauk Pass, Arakan, 1942.

Silence,
only silence now,
except for charred trees
hissing in the dew-drenched dawn.
No other morn
was born so desolated,
nor orchestrated
with such trembling breathless emptiness.

They stand, now,
these dying blistered trees,
like smouldering spectral victims of the longest night,
and they bleed with swollen tears of molten sap,
in ghastly sillhouette against the growing light,
like gaunt defeated sentinels,
naked in the morning mist,
vanquished,
slain,
alone,
death-kissed.

What else?
Who else has this night's havoc
drained full sap of life, -
or left with searing scars,
the strewn largesse of strife?

Clifford Leeming

192

Requiem for the Mother's Child
(After Dalton Trumbo's 'Johnny got his Gun')

Your truth is pain greater
than death, Johnny. The narrow
cot does promise oblivion
and you, featured in all the tortured
faces, know the comfort of that.

But Johnny, the waste...

They planted poppies in your
eyes. The bright, bitter petals
spilt and pooled, dousing your
light - we see the splintered space
of trees recycled into cruciform,
now that science is prepared
for its own begotten son to reap
all the flowers of the field

you lost your chance
of music - we hear the clamouring
of usury; the discordancy
of madness giggling at its own joke.

Then what of hope - must
it be left to the knife, as the last
fit tool to scratch
the persistently itching crotch?

Ah Johnny, to think

that in a world such as this
should be, there could
be anything worse than death.

Brenda Whincup

Who Will Remember

Remembrance Day is every day for me and countless others.
Remembrance of those bloody days, when we stood and fought as
brothers.
United by a common bond, a common aim to save,
This land we love, its freedom, and all our strength we gave.
And with the dawn of each new day, we live again the fight.
Remembering the friends who fell, and forever in our sight.

Scant was the glory in those days, whilst we struggled to survive.
The days and nights were horror-filled, and we prayed to stay alive.
And each day we remember, the reek of fear and blood.
The dead of every Army, sprawled in dust and mud.
Khaki, grey, green and red, the colours vivid, dead.
And we hear again the piteous cried, of the wounded as they bled.

Then on the single sorrow-day, when our Nation mourns its dead.
We see the standards fluttering, the wreaths all poppies, red.
And we march again with comrades, proud at having served,
Remembering those who'd fallen, and weep silent, unobserved.
We hear the prayers, stand quiet, respecting all the dead.
Responding, 'we will remember them', when Binyon's verse is read.

But when the day has ended, the bugles slung, and stilled,
And poppy flowers lie dying, symbolic of those killed.
The prayers all said, parades dismissed, the medals stored away.
We who served, and now are old, recalling each war day.
Must wonder who, in this proud land, when we have passed away,
Will say, 'we will remember them', on Remembrance Day.

Graham Lewis

Old Soldier

Up and over, brave men paced to strife.
Lines of humanity on that hot, summer dawn,
To destiny walked with rifles, bayonets drawn.
How great is this feeling for the warriors life,
With no thoughts of money, children or wife.
Bravado changed to terror as death swept the plain,
Shell, bomb or bullet killed, left minds insane.
I know, I lived where the heaped dead were rife.

Years have passed since I walked with the brave,
Old wounds are hurting, both legs are lame.
Now life moves forward, sedentary and tame,
And I worry. Of money in banks, put by to save,
Of shopping lists and outside the path, to pave.
I hear comrades calling softly in the night,
To meet again and march forward to fight.
And sometimes I wish I'd a soldiers grave.

Richard Malcolm Harding

Thoughts on the Frustration of War

Times change;
And seconds flit about my finger tips;
To fall in waste eternity.
Ash from my cigarette
Becomes immortal dust! as sunsual man
Creates, in wanton lust, His likeness,
That it might also rest upon the evergreen.
This negative of time
Fused in a past and future atmosphere
Awaiteth man to change the tense
- Awaiteth man's aoristic phase -
Then smiles and yesterday is born.
What purpose life if Caesar's fault
Lays bare the womb of future's infertility:
This orb of dust, pinioned in space
Poised in the spiral of eternity,
These images of Christ, this race of clay,
Elated in mortality.
The trickling sand stays not to hold
Love's freedom to my thirsting lips.
All then is lost and hope mere hopelessness
As ally and foe render paternal prayers
For victory, to that same God
Who made the serpent to entwine the truth.

India 1945

W K Cork

The Sacrifice

If I should not return, if 'tis my lot
To be among the war's unnumbered dead;
To lie in some shell-hole, by men forgot,
No simple cross to mark the place where rest my head;

If this proud form ruled by a prouder mind
Should return to dust from whence it came,
And reluctantly leave this world behind:
In the supreme sacrifice find undying fame:

If this warm, rich red blood of mine should flow,
And some far distant alien soil imbrue,
I trust you will never forget the debt you owe,
But remember I died for freedom, and for you.

Wilf Farries

Buttercup Gold

The old man walked the country lanes
Eyes misted by time and rimmed with tears.
Long ago memories still fresh and new,
As he walked back through the years.

These meadows now clothed in buttercup gold,
Where once the trenches had been.
The sounds of spring drifting on the breeze
Replacing the gunfire and screams.

The gleaming medals he wore on his chest
Radiated his innermost pride.
They told of the campaigns and battles of old
And the comrades who'd fought by his side.

The years had gone by, not faded by time,
And his pals still marched by his side.
Was it worth the price they'd willingly paid;
They'd fought - but why had they died.

All those years ago the world seemed to end
In this very same countryside.
But who could tell, looking at this scene
That a whole generation had died.

H Atkinson

Italy 1944

Of Father time! What have you done
Why tilt your glass for us so young?
Your scythe has taken all the best.
Hardly fresh from Mothers breast
Virgin boys of tender years.
Tumbling through the vale of tears,
Friend and Foe alike
Joined together by human blight,
The vicious burst of Bren and Spandau gun
Blotting out their youthful sun
Not as bad as their Fathers war
But dead is dead and they laugh no more.

L G Mayhew

Remembrance

Marching feet are fading away,
young men are leaving our shores today.
Not all will return, some will stay.
Buried under foreign clay.

Tears are falling like drops of blood,
falling from a gaping wound.
They're falling for those loved one who stay
Buried under foreign clay.

Hearts are beating, some too painfully.
Beating out a sad and endless refrain.
Too sad to cry, just wondering why
Those we love had to die.

In silence we stand on Remembrance Day,
Bowing hour heads to quietly pray.
Now they come they are here to stay.
These men have escaped the foreign clay.

Pauline Louise Cousins

A Posthumous Medal

As the soldiers marched away
And the tanks rolled out of sight
the flag was slowly lowered
The lonely piper, played on into the night
His music was soft and low
The tune was mournful and sad
A posthumous medal lay on a satin bed
Of a brave young soldier lad.
Tears have flowed in torrents
From relatives and his girlfriend
Only eighteen years of age
His war was just pretend
Blanks and fire crackers
Noisily blowing in the wind
His first day in battle
And to the ground he was pinned
He knew nothing of the Ministers and Generals
And they knew even less of him
But this my friend is war
And not parading all neat and trim
One soldier dies
Another takes his place
A name, a number and a memory left
No-one, saw his face.

Lawrence McGranaghan

The Unknown Warrior:

Here lies the debt of our proud nation
Albion's man who died to keep her free
Joined in battle with her enemies
Shed his blood for you and me.

Here lies the son of every Mother
The Husband of every sorrowing Wife
The Father of every orphaned child
Who in that war gave up his life.

Here lies the hope of all our children
Peace to erase the Mark of Cain
That on the battle fields of flanders
This warrior's death was not in vain.

Here lies mortality in splendour
Brought home from a foreign grave
With Kings and Queens forever sleeping
In the Abbey's hallowed nave.

Alan Knill

D Day

Small landing craft, their bottoms flat
Were built for calmer seas
The soldiers thrown from stem to stern
Were sick, and ill at ease

The 'Ben Mcree' was in the fleet
Red crosses large and clear
Young men fell silent at the sight
The time to die was near

The airborne struck at dead of night
With orders to secure
The coastal guns, some miles inland
And make the landings sure

Snipers hiding in a steeple
Or strapped into a tree
Spread fear and panic all around
A killer one can't see

The lad ahead steps on a mine
At once he knows the score
His thoughts are for the ones he loved
And then is no more

Two tiger tanks ahead of us
Cause our advance to slow
Until the Typhoons shoot them up
And we are free to go

Young men on both sides feel that day
Theirs not to reason why
But one truth stands above all else
They were too young to die

Roy Bennett

Before my Eyes

Before my eyes red-rimmed and sore,
Battle weary, from night before.
I stare at dawn from that bloody trench,
See the death, and smell the stench.
Of bodies open, stiff and torn,
By bullet, mortar, blast and mine.
Life-less, staring at the sky,
Or, lying peaceful, glad to die.
Lips cracked and dry, lice in hair,
Dirty and weary, I stand to stare.
To see the scene I saw before,
Wondering why, I was spared once more.
Perhaps quite soon, throughout that day,
Or at least by dusk or night.
I too ... may lie amongst the dead,
After giving up the fight.
And some else's red-rimmed eye's
Will look at dawn ... and see that sight.

M Kerkhoff

Suburban Shelter

Sirens wailed up and down -
black-out, midnight.

Sisters huddled, hauled from bed,
eiderdowns cuddled,

Shivering, shaking, down the dark garden
parent led,

Stumbling, mumbling, even grumbling
hiding fear.

Hastening to-wards the secret shelter
like a badger's lair,

Hidden under a hillock beneath the trees
deceptively.

Handed down cold concrete steps
reluctantly,

Holding each other, comrades forever
in that earthly cover.

Chattering teeth, chapped chilled hands
clutching Mother.

Cowering in the dark dungeon, listening - listening
to unearthy silence,

Clinging together and waiting - waiting -
waiting for the end.

Crying out in a fit of frozen fury
'Let me die in bed!'

Sheila Bone

To our Gurkha and Indian Comrades-In-Arms

Their native land no more they'll see
A white stone marks their grave,
They gave their lives for Britain,
Those lives they scorned to save,
From the Himalayan foothills,
And India's sunny plains,
They sent their finest regiments
To conquer, and regain
Lands taken by an enemy
Whose overwhelming might
Turned the darkening clouds of warfare
Into everlasting night.
To you, brave dusky warriors
Our eternal thanks are due,
And when we wear our poppy,
We'll be thinking Pals, of you

R Cherrill

The Night They Bombed Augusta

That night we lay in camp upon a hill
above Catania, and were at ease
beneath the sky. Untiring in the trees
sleepless cicadas sang, all singing still
for dead Theocritus. We drank our fill
of heady muscatel, and watch'd the seas
turn wine-dark in the dusk - where Ulysses
forever homeward ran, and ever will.

That night they bomb'd Augusta. Overhead,
careless of us, the planes went droning by.
We saw the flares go drifting down - pell mell
the flak go racing up - the sky turn red
where suns rise not nor set. In Heaven high
that night we lay - and watch'd men burn in Hell!

F Forrester

Untitled

Pull down your visor Pilot
I can not look you in the eyes.
Yet I share your apprehension
As you fly those eastern skies.
So remain a faceless warrior,
It will help me with my fear.
Combat my shame and ease my guilt,
For you are there, while I am here.
I hope you see tomorrows sun
And share the chores of life,
I Wonder at your courage
And I pray for your children and wife.
So pull down your visor pilot
As one of the chosen few,
Defend your Queen and countrymen,
And may our God be ever with you.

Colin McCombe

Lucky Boys

Righto lads get off your bums,
We've got a job to do,
They've stopped the 'Queens' just up the road,
Our job's to get them through.

We mounted up, got on our way,
Flag down and go like hell,
The first lot packed it in quite quick,
They'd had it, you could tell.

They hoisted up their hands at once,
We didn't fire a shot,
We sent 'em marching down the road,
A surprised and sorry lot.

Then away again in a cloud of dust,
And fired on from the right,
We saw this lot were holed up,
In a building out of sight.

We swanned around that building,
Giving it all we'd got,
Grenades through every window,
Besa, Sten the lot.

Then the door burst open,
And out those Jerries ran,
It was just that time my bloody Sten,
Decided it would jam.

Luck was with me, and with them,
'Cos both put up their hands,
I guess their lives were saved that day,
By a bit of dust or sand.

I often think with pleasure,
That fate stepped in just then,
Like me, maybe, they're Grandads,
Another forty years to spend.

L/Cpl Albert Bell 1st Fife and Forfars Yeomaniy

Gratitude - 1914 - 1918

I heard the bugle calling and rallied round the flag,
and marching with my comrades I sang 'Your old kit-bag'.

I fought in every great campaign that held the foe at bay,
and watched my friends diminish as they perished day by day.

Some were shot, others gassed, some blown to bits by shell,
but Lady Luck smiled down on me and guided me through hell.

Today I'm just a crippled tramp with medals on my chest,
the Retreat from Mons - the Dardanelles - the Somme - and all the
rest.

And those I saved now pass me by, like they might a plague or pest,
and when they do I oft-times wish I'd perished with the rest.

John Morrison

Ten

I was ten, when it was 'then', in 1939,
In ignorance and innocence I thought that things were fine,
Then it came, that call-up time, for dads to go to war,
And one of them was mine.

I felt the fear a child can know, the insecure hate,
of Dunkirk that Dad was in,
Whilst we were left to wait,
Worried and uncertain about his fate.

He came through, yet not for long was he home to stay,
To the Middle East, soon he was on his way.
At home, the anxiety, the bombings night and day,
When it would be over, nobody could say.

In '45 it ended, and he returned across the sea,
But the stranger who came home, was the Dad I couldn't see,
Through the eyes of a stranger, that was also me,
For time decreed as ever, ten I couldn't be.

Forever gone, the child he loved and knew,
A teenager, the child years were so few
And it would never be the same, though we would wish it to,
For what has happened in the past, we never can un-do.

It is now, the years have flown, grandaughters have I two,
One is eight and one is ten, the age when I went through,
What they, thank God, never knew, the time
When I was ten, and it was 'then', in 1939.

Iris Gunner